"Read My Lips: No New Taxes"

Dan Ostrander

George Bush

– Photo by Dan Ostrander, May 8, 1989, The White House

"READ MY LIPS: NO NEW TAXES"

BY

DAN OSTRANDER

FOREWORD

BY

GEORGE BUSH

Butte College Press
3565 Butte Campus Drive
Oroville, California 95965

ISBN 0-9632909-6-7

Library of Congress Card Number: 00-102854

First Trade Edition

CONTENTS

Chapter IV: George Bush's related Speeches/Press Conferences

ACKNOWLEDGEMENTS

In gathering the information for this book I have drawn from public papers and interviews. I would like to thank both Presidents Bush and Ford for their time and participation. A special thanks is due President Bush's chief of staff, Jean Becker, for her efforts and constant support. For their valuable input, my gratitude is also extended to Richard Darman, Director of the OMB under President Bush; former House Speaker, Thomas Foley; and Joe Coyne Director of Public Affairs, Federal Reserve Board.

I have been aided in the preparation, research, writing, and editing of this book by many people, but I would like to thank a special few: Dawn Hawkins, Mark Alcorn, Bob Suschil, Margaret Hughes, and Josh Cook.

FOREWORD

P rofessor Ostrander has spent several years researching and compiling this book, which largely deals with what has become known as the "1990 Budget Deal." After very painful and tedious negotiations with the Democrat-controlled Congress, my administration hammered out a budget agreement (HR 5835 – PL 101-508) that included budget cuts and a tax increase of almost $500 billion (over five years). Most important, however, in the budget agreement were changes that drastically altered the budget process that Congress had followed. This package of procedural changes was designed to make the budget savings stick by establishing a new "pay-as-you-go" system, enforceable caps on discretionary spending, and extending the Gramm-Rudman-Hollings sequester process by the use of mini-sequesters. Along the way, I lost the support of many people in my own party, and also had to break my pledge of "no new taxes" from the 1988 campaign. Although, I knew at the time I was taking a huge political risk, I thought getting the deficit down, continuing economic expansion, and employment in this country were more important than my earlier campaign pledge not to raise taxes; thus our budget agreement was in the best interests of the country.

There were times when even I questioned the success of my

own economic program. I even stated publicly that I had made a mistake because raising taxes was such a painful thing to do and because the benefits of the deficit reduction process took much longer to become evident than I or anyone on my staff had hoped.

Many political pundits believe that the deal did contribute to my defeat in 1992, which was quite painful. However, as the current economy continues to grow and now that we have a balanced budget, I have been gratified by the many economists and elected officials who partially credit what we did in 1990 for the reason the economy is so healthy now. We took a huge gamble then and it's nice to see the payoffs now.

This book helps clarify and explain the effects of the "1990 Budget Deal" and I am grateful to Professor Ostrander for tackling this very complicated task of explaining one of the most controversial events of my Presidency. I admit I am flattered by his conclusion. Mostly, I hope this book will give the reader some insight into the art of negotiation and compromise and our system of government at work.

George Bush

INTRODUCTION

"READ MY LIPS"

Political Pragmatism: an Essential Ingredient for Effective Presidential Leadership

Like President Franklin D. Roosevelt (FDR) who used political pragmatism rather than ideology to guide this nation through the greatest economic crises of the first half of the twentieth century, President George Bush should also be remembered as a pragmatic leader who had the **vision** to see that the nation's growing deficit could have created the greatest economic crisis of the second-half of the twentieth century. Not only did Bush have the vision to see the emerging deficit problem, he also had the political will and discipline to guide this nation through it. His leadership stabilized the economy and established the economic framework of deficit reduction, enforceable caps on federal discretionary spending, and a pay-as-you-go budget policy. This framework became the **key to economic recovery** that will carry this country into the twenty-first century.

Bush's economic leadership was not based on any single economic theory or ideology but rather a **pragmatic balancing act** between the needs of the nation and what he could get from a Democratically controlled Congress and the conservative wing of his own party. Bush did not practice pragmatism as an end in itself. For him it was only a tool of effective leadership to make the impossible possible in order to make a difference for the people and this nation. Like FDR, what mattered most to George Bush was people. His vision, as expressed in his "thousand points of light"* concept, was that public service gave him as well as others the opportunity to provide an environment for people to have security and opportunity. Without **vision,** pragmatism is impotent and is nothing more than splitting the difference between extremes or taking the middle ground as an easy way out. Bush was not the kind of public servant who looked for the easy way out; he looked for the right way out. Bush's clarity of thought and his quick and decisive actions in dealing with the S & L debacle within his first sixteen days in office,** the Persian Gulf War, and the structural budget deficit problem he inherited from the previous administration all demonstrate this point.

Balance and pragmatism are the key words for understanding George Bush. Like FDR during the Great Depression, who had to balance the social needs of society against that of a free enterprise system, George Bush had to balance and integrate the social needs of a more complex society against the need to establish **long-term** economic growth. The strategic issue for Bush was how to formulate an economic policy for the country that would give short-term economic and political nourishment, while at the same time satisfying the country's **long-term** economic and social needs. In times of crisis, in order for the needs of the country to be met, there

---

*"I have spoken of a thousand points of light, of all the community organizations that are spread like stars throughout the Nation, doing good. We will work hand in hand, encouraging, sometimes leading, sometimes being led, rewarding. We will work on this in the White House, in the Cabinet agencies. I will go to the people and the programs that are the brighter points of light, and I will ask every member of my government to become involved. The old ideas are new again because they are not old; they are timeless: duty, sacrifice, commitment, and a patriotism that finds its expression in taking part and pitching in."
(See Section IV, Page 103 for Inaugural Address, January 20, 1989)

**With S & L failures out of control and showing every sign of growing worse, Bush announced a plan to clean up the mess and signed into law the Financial Institutions Reform Recovery and Enforcement Act on February 6, 1989.

is a need for a President to demonstrate good governance by making a conscious choice between what is in the best interest of the country over successful political policy or good politics. This choice of good governance over good politics is often ignored and unappreciated.

It is widely believed that Bush made a political mistake when he uttered the famous sound bite, "Read my lips: no new taxes" yet subsequently reached a budget agreement with Congress to raise taxes. Bush's failure to win reelection in 1992 seems to reinforce this belief promoted by his critics. However, his defeat was caused by numerous factors, only one of which was the public's false perception about the state of the economy. Bush did not allow his no new tax pledge to reduce his will or capacity for **good governance.** The litmus test for the actions of President Bush, or any President, is found in the answers to the following questions: (1) Was Bush's renunciation of his no new tax pledge a mistake against the best interests of the country in favor of personal, political, or party interests? (2) Did the renunciation violate the integrity of the office of the Presidency? (3) Did this renunciation violate his own personal integrity?†

The answer to these questions is NO. Bush was responding to a grave economic crisis of high projected deficits and increases in long-term interest rates, which threatened future economic growth and productivity and could have created a possible sequestration.‡ The problems with the economy were also exacerbated by the spike in oil prices caused by Saddam Hussein's actions in the summer of 1990. If Bush failed to reduce the deficit by reach-

---

† Throughout the introduction the word President is spelled with a capital "P" to give the office of the Presidency equal footing with Congress.

‡ In 1985 Congress passed the Gramm-Rudman-Hollings Deficit Reduction Act which initially required that the deficit be cut to specific levels each year until it reached zero in 1991. The Act stated that if Congress and the White House could not agree on a plan that would bring the deficit in on target in any given year, automatic across-the-board spending cuts would take place, a process called sequestration.

ing an agreement with Congress, he would have possibly triggered automatic cuts in funds for defense, because of the sequestration process, at the very time he was asking the Department of Defense to prepare for possible war with Saddam Hussein in the Persian Gulf. Consequently, not only for domestic economic stability, but also so the United States could contribute to world peace by helping stabilizing the Persian Gulf region, Bush had no choice but to negotiate the best agreement he could with a Democratically controlled Congress. The Congress insisted upon a tax increase as part of any deficit reduction agreement. Bush's response in raising taxes went against his own political beliefs and interest. He did what he felt was in the best interest of the country and thereby upheld the integrity of the office of the Presidency as well as his own personal integrity.

> It's a tough decision, it's not an easy decision I've made, but it is the right decision.... But I'm in here to do what is best for the country; and what is best for the country is to get this deficit under control, to get this economy moving again, and to see people at jobs, not out on some welfare line. And that's what's at stake here – economic soundness of the United States. *(See Chapter IV, Page 175 for the October 6,1990, Press Conference on the Federal Budget Crisis).*

A President should care more about the country than he does for himself. He must put the interest of the country above his own political beliefs, and he must have the **vision** to recognize when his beliefs are incongruent with the interest of the country. If a President falls prey to the political pressures within his party or society and compromises himself or what he believes to be right in his conscience for the sake of successful political policy, then he has failed himself, the office of the Presidency, and most important of all, he has failed the people who elected him to use his judgement to represent their interests. Bush's concern for good public policy instead of good political policy, is an example of effective Presidential leadership.

In evaluating the famous "Read my lips: no new taxes" statement made by Bush in his acceptance speech at the Republican National Convention on August 18, 1988, *(See Chapter IV, Page 120)* several significant features of Presidential leadership must be understood. The key principles behind effective Presidential leadership are best understood when viewed within an historical perspective. This perspective helps avoid the passions of contemporary politics. Without this perspective we as citizens will fall prey to the demagoguery of the media and the political process and lose sight of what is truly in the national interest. Hence, the purpose of this book is to put Bush's actions into this historical perspective so that they may be properly evaluated and appreciated. The book is a "profile in courage" on the Presidency, in that it examines the actions of Jefferson, Lincoln, and Ford to demonstrate their political character. This "profile in courage" approach is used in an effort to educate the reader to an important and often overlooked aspect of Presidential leadership: political pragmatism. Thus, the book, is divided into four distinct sections: the first briefly covers the characteristics of Presidential leadership; the second discusses the historical parallels of three past Presidents who demonstrated great Presidential leadership by **good governance** through pragmatism; the third discusses the background and the political conditions surrounding the budget agreement made between President Bush and Congress; and the fourth presents the relevant speeches and the press conferences of President George Bush during the 1990 budget crisis.

CHAPTER I

PRESIDENTIAL LEADERSHIP

Even though this section does not provide a comprehensive theory of the Presidency on domestic policy, it does provide some of the key factors that must be understood to properly evaluate the actions of the modern President by keeping in mind the true character of the office. The framers of the Constitution did not conceive of the Presidency as the focus of leadership, but only planned for the President to be the administrative head of the new federal government. But today, Presidents have vastly extended their leadership capacities with their influence in legislative leadership, party leadership, public opinion, morals and global-strategy. The key question is how much power has the office of the Presidency really gained? Today, for most Americans, the President is the focal point of public life. Underlying their view of the Presidency is a common assumption that the President should be the leader in solving America's domestic problems as well as the problems of an increasingly interdependent world. Public perception of what the President should do, however, often exceeds his real power. This section explores the potential power of the President as well as the boundaries that limit that power.

A. The Image of the Presidency

Understanding how the image of the office of the Presidency as well as the image of the person holding the office can expand and contract Presidential power is important to understanding Presidential leadership. The image of the Presidency will be viewed from four different perspectives: (1) the image the President himself has of the office, (2) the image the public has of the office and the person holding the office, (3) the image Congress has of the President and the office, and (4) the image the media creates of the person holding the office as well as the office itself.

The **image a President has of the office** will either expand or contract his powers as President. Franklin D. Roosevelt's concept of the Presidency was: "pre-eminently a place of moral leadership." Theodore Roosevelt (TR) once defined his concept of the President as "steward of the people" and held that "it was not only his right but his duty to do anything that the needs of the nation demanded unless such action was forbidden by the Constitution or by the laws." Theodore Roosevelt lived up to his concept of the Presidency and is looked upon by historians as one of our more successful Presidents. William Howard Taft, who does not command the same respect by historians as the Roosevelts and succeeded TR in the Presidency, believed he could exercise only those Presidential powers derived from a strict reading of the Constitution or those given to him by an act of Congress. He scoffed at the idea of some "undefined residuum of power" that a President can exercise "because it seems to him to be in the public interest."

Jimmy Carter's concept of the Presidency, although legislatively aggressive, was much humbler in style than either of the two Roosevelts. Carter, like FDR, saw himself as a moral leader for the people and like TR, also saw himself as a guardian of the people's interests against special interest groups, particularly those found in Congress. The difference between the Roosevelts and Carter was that Carter's political style ran into difficultly with the media and the general public when he tried to develop a "political form" that created a humbler image of the Presidency. By adopting different symbolic gestures during his term of office, such as carrying his own bags when traveling or using the nickname "Jimmy," Carter made the **office and himself** seem less awesome and in turn less Presidential. The consequences of Carter's humble concept of the Presidency was he came to be portrayed as a man who literally and figuratively lacked stature and was dwarfed by his responsibilities. Although Carter was a better President than the media and general public give him credit for, what is learned from Carter's experience is that the media's impact can turn appearances into reality. Carter reduced the powerful image of the "imperial Presidency" to the image of the humble Presidency. Although humility is an admirable quality, the simple fact is that Presidential power is enhanced by the appearance of infallibility and invincibility, not humility.

From the public's perspective, the collective heritage of the office of the Presidency and the "textbook" view* of the President as the primary policy-maker in the American political system has led to the development of unrealistic images and expectations by the public of the office holder. This collective heritage begins with George Washington. It was the Founding Fathers' idea to find a man in America who could represent the virtues of the people and who had the character and leadership style to formalize the new political institutions. It was hoped that George Washington's reputation and character would draw the different political factions together so that they might overcome their personal interests in favor of the best interest of the new nation. Today the general public and the media sustain this view of the Presidency as an office with the ability to deliver the nation from danger as a result of its occupants' greatness. It is widely believed that the institution of the Presidency has the potential to make extraordinary events happen and that the occupant should be able to realize that potential. Thus, historically, Presidents personify the government and make

---

*The term "textbook" Presidency was coined by Thomas Cronin in his book *The State of the Presidency* (1975). It refers to the idealized view of the President presented in introductory high school and college textbooks as the only one who can affect positive change in American government and policy. It also implies that the President should be the nation's personal and moral leader and that the electoral system will produce the right person for the job.

it possible for the general public to be engaged by what otherwise would be an impersonal abstraction. However, this impersonal abstraction has consequence which has created an historical paradox. A President must play into the high and unrealistic images and expectations the general public has of him because by playing into these images the President enhances his ability to make his policies become a reality. Yet, simultaneously, he contributes to a public atmosphere that blames him alone for problems he alone cannot solve; consequently, if either the economy or the government fails to meet popular expectations, the President takes the blame.

Another example of a President's need to shape images and expectations is found with the Carter Presidency. Carter's attempt to accomplish more than was politically possible resulted in high expectations. After his election, Carter arrived in Washington with a full agenda of campaign promises he expected to carry out. Because he emphasized the President's role as the moral leader for the American people, the public also expected him to implement his agenda. What were these many programs on the Carter agenda during his first year? The list was exhaustive. It included creation of a Department of Energy, a comprehensive energy program, strip-mining controls, reauthorization of the clean air program, an omnibus farm and food program (including food stamps), increase in the minimum wage, welfare reform, creation of an agency for consumer protection, hospital cost containment, Social Security financing, an economic stimulus program, reduction in water projects, reauthorization of the water pollution control programs, housing and urban aid proposals, and restoring the President's reorganization authority in order to reform many government functions. Carter also wanted to reduce the deficit and to balance the budget. When some of these goals were not met, or were not met with the speed Carter had projected, he was judged an ineffective leader. In contrast, Reagan's limited agenda raised fewer expectations, most of which were met, thus creating the image of Reagan as an effective leader. This successful image gave Reagan more political capital to accomplish future goals with Congress.

A President must not only cultivate an effective image with the general public, but he must also maintain a similar **image with Congress.** If a President appears to be inept or disinterested in handling congressional relations, critics will probably find fault with his legislative performance. This is particularly true for a President like Carter with no congressional experience and little sensitivity to the institutional norms of Congress or to its members' sense of politics for the benefit of their constituencies. Especially disconcerting to members of Congress is the tendency of Presidents to shift positions quickly without consulting Congressional leaders or lawmakers. In cases involving important issues to the nation, their state, or district, lawmakers feel they need to give input and, if necessary, they need time to make political adjustments to the new change in public policy. An example of such congressional frustration with Carter and a reason why Bush was unsuccessful in passing his first budget agreement on October 5, 1990, is found in the following quote from Stuart Eizenstat, President Carter's domestic policy adviser:

> You can't try to short-circuit it (the political system). You can't assume that a small group of leaders has to get together and cut deals to impose on the system. When you do that, as Bush did with the budget summit, you end up with a situation in which the political system can't digest the package because it was never a party to it. That's why Carter's 1977 energy program got rejected – it was a bolt out of the blue.

During the 1990 budget agreement, some members of Congress felt the lack of an effective liaison between key members of the Bush Administration and Congress contributed to the defeat of the first budget agreement. Because Congressional leaders can prevent the President from realizing his goals, the significance of an effective congressional liaison office cannot be overstated. This office, which can explain and promote the President's position, is an essential component of the modern Presidency.

The Eisenhower administration formalized **modern** Presidential relations with Congress by establishing the Congressional Liaison Office. The function of the liaison office is to provide information to members of Congress, to conduct Presidential bargaining with Congress, to lobby for Presidential proposals through explanation and low-key persuasion, and to help with constituency-related matters. Operational staff, who maintain daily contact with members of Congress, are assigned to either the House or the Senate. The Congressional Liaison Office is also important because Presidents can only count on their own party members for support no more than two-thirds of the time; hence, Presidents must build coalitions by obtaining support from members of the opposition party. A frequent condition that makes coalition building especially important is opposition control of one or both houses of Congress. On many occasions, Presidents have received crucial support from the opposition. Several factors other than party membership influence congressional voting decisions: constituency pressures, state and regional loyalty, ideological orientations, and the influence of interest groups. The President's liaison office can use these factors to enhance the President's influence.

A final factor in dealing with a President's ability to influence Congress is called the "law of anticipated reaction." Members of Congress do what they think they must do in order to survive, and a President's affect on them is heightened or diminished by their thoughts about his anticipated reaction to their action. What they expect of a President becomes a cardinal factor in his power to persuade them. To maximize his prospects for effectiveness, a President must concern himself with what others think. When members of Congress consider their relationship with the President it does them little good to scan the Constitution or remind themselves that Presidents possess potential vantage points which they lack. Instead, they anticipate, as best they can, the President's ability and will to make use of his bargaining advantages. Out of what others think of him emerge his opportunities for influence with them. Signs of tenacity count as much as signs of skill in shaping expectations of a President's behavior. Effective power is therefore based upon establishing a reputation of tenacity that will withstand the shocks of daily disruptions and obstructions by various entities within society and will transmit this impression to the public as well as to the minds of Washingtonians-at-large.

This "law of anticipated reaction" and political tenacity is best illustrated by the actions of President Ronald Reagan during the air traffic controllers strike. On August 3, 1981, more than 85 percent of the members of the Professional Air Traffic Controllers Organization (PATCO) went on strike across the United States despite repeated warnings by Reagan that any controller who refused to work would be fired. At the time of the strike, public opinion was supportive of public employees striking. Government negotiators had offered a compromise settlement, but it was judged unacceptable by the union. PATCO's demands included a four-day thirty two hour work week, a $10,000 across-the board raise, and additional retirement benefits. The union was found in contempt of court and fined $250,000 for the first three days and $1 million a day thereafter. Meanwhile, some 2,000 nonstriking PATCO members and an equal number of nonunion controllers manned the towers with the help of supervisory personnel. The botched strike showed that the PATCO leadership had badly overrated the effect of their endorsement of Reagan in the 1980 campaign, ignored his often stated revulsion against strikes by federal employees, and erroneously expected the strike to create chaos in the skies. As a result, 12,000 men and women lost their jobs and Reagan's firm action sent shock waves through the ranks of organized labor. By the time the strike was over, public opinion opposed public employees striking. At the same time, Reagan's public image and political capital with Congress and the general public had increased tremendously. Reagan later stated in his autobiography, "I think it convinced people who might have thought otherwise that I meant what I said."

In conclusion, Presidential success requires consultation before and during legislative consideration and a willingness to negotiate and bargain with Congress. Coordination of legislative proposals between the White House and the departments and agencies is essential. More important, cooperation between the President and Congressional leaders and between the institutional Presidency and Congress is mandatory. The constitutional separation of powers does not allow the two branches to operate independently of each other; rather, it requires that they exercise their shared powers jointly.

The final issue in understanding the image of the Presidency is the **image the media creates** of the office. At a minimum, democracy requires that citizens receive objective information so they can make informed decisions about candidates, policies, and government actions. Because most citizens draw their conclusions about politics from the information given to them by the media, the images the media creates become extremely important. In order to understand and to appreciate the lessons of our historical heritage and to avoid the passions of the media and contemporary politics, the positive and negative influences of the media over the course of American history must be understood.

The importance of the media in American politics dates from the pre-revolutionary war period when newspapers served as the most important tool for disseminating ideas and mobilizing public opinion. Although the newspapers were the most important means of communication, they were more or less tools for popular leaders like Samuel Adams and James Otis in Boston, Charles Thomson and Thomas Paine in Philadelphia, and Richard Henry Lee and Patrick Henry of Virginia. With direction from these popular leaders, American unity from the Stamp Act of 1765 on was promoted by newspaper accounts of what the other colonies were doing; thus, Massachusetts was prodded into action by newspaper reports of Patrick Henry's Stamp Act resolves in the Virginia House of Burgesses and the need for a Continental Congress was fully debated in the press long before it was actually convened. Hence, the significance of the media during this period was that it provided unity in ideas and purpose within the American colonies against the British.

During the period before the Civil War, the media played an equally important role in bringing about the war. From 1846 though 1860 the emotional and psychological make-up of both the North and South were turned into political hysteria by the media as it exploited sectional stories and created stereotypical views for both sections that were unrealistic and very damaging to the political process. These stereotypical views made it impossible for the two sides to settle their differences.

This process is best exemplified by *Uncle Tom's Cabin* written by Harriet Beecher Stowe in 1851. Published in an antislavery magazine over a ten-month period, *Uncle Tom's Cabin* was the most celebrated publication of its time. In 1852, due to popular demand, it was published in book form. Its net effect was to inflame one-half of the nation against the other; it helped produce disunion and civil war by **giving people an image** of slavery which was not universally correct. The book did so by using the emotions of various heart-breaking episodes of slavery. The fact that Mrs. Stowe had never personally observed slavery did not harm the sale of the novel.

The importance of *Uncle Tom's Cabin* lay not in whether it was an accurate account of the institution of slavery. Rather, the novel was important because it supplied Northerners with concrete stereotypes which helped intensify sectional conflict and made communication between themselves and Southerners very difficult. When Lincoln met Mrs. Stowe during the War his comment to her was, "So you are the little lady who started this great war."

Another historical example of the media's impact can be seen with the election of Jimmy Carter in 1976. In January 1976, the Gallop Poll stated Carter had the support of only four percent of the Democratic voters. In February, after winning the New Hampshire primary, he jumped to 12 percent. By the third week in March (after the Florida primary), he jumped to 26 percent. The question then being asked by the media was, *"Can Anybody Stop Jimmy Carter Now?" (U.S. News and World Report, 3/29/76)*.

By mid-March 1976, Carter was far ahead of the active contenders for the Democratic Presidential nomination and led President Ford by a few percentage points. In the space of only a few months, Jimmy Carter was transformed from a virtual unknown to one of the most popular politicians in the entire nation. He became as popular as men who had been prominent in national politics for decades. The reason for his astonishing rise was not only found in Carter's message to the American people, but in the media's reporting of the events which portrayed Carter as the right man, at the right time, and in the right place. Carter's message of moral leadership was historically timely with events like the Vietnam War, Watergate, and Nixon's pardon dominating the political landscape. Carter's victory over Ford in 1976 was possible because the media portrayed Carter as the candidate most in touch with the character and morals of the American people. At the same time, the media portrayed Ford as an incompetent bungler, who carried the odor of Watergate because of his pardon of Nixon. The media overreacted to the pardon, claiming a deal had been made and paid little attention to Ford's explanation for the pardon. The press raised questions about Ford's character instead of his judgment, confirming in the minds of most Americans the image of immorality in Washington and within the Republican Party; thus, the press created an atmosphere which enhanced Carter's image as a moral crusader. The interpretative focus the media puts on events can be critical. The media's focus on Carter's character and moral leadership, versus Ford's pardon of Nixon, made Carter's timing very effective.

Besides helping Carter with his victory over Ford, the press also helped Carter win the Democratic Presidential nomination in 1976 by emphasizing his victories and putting a positive spin on his defeats. On June 8, Super Tuesday, primaries were held in California, New Jersey and Ohio. On that date, 540 delegates, more than a third of the total needed for the nomination, were selected. *The New York Times* front-page story about New Jersey on the day before the primary read, *"Carter Victory Is Forecast in Jersey Vote Tomorrow."* When Carter gained only 25 of the 108 delegates in

New Jersey, the Times front-page headline on Thursday proclaimed, *"Carter Seems Due to Win on First Ballot."* At the same time, there was a story on page 43 entitled, *"Humphrey-Brown Victory in Jersey Is Called Futile."* The fact that Carter lost in California and New Jersey was not addressed; what became the major story of the day was that he won in Ohio. In terms of fairness to both the candidates and the public, the Ohio story should have been balanced by the New Jersey and California outcomes, yet it was not done. The press's image of "Carter the winner" contributed to the bandwagon effect that pushed Carter to victory at the Democratic Convention.

This selective process exerted by the media over public opinion is called "gate keeping." An explanation for this type of gate keeping can be found in the media's desire to reflect its personal values by making one candidate an attractive winner and another a humiliated loser. Other explanations are the media's inability or unwillingness to explain the complexity of the campaign issues, as well as, its desire to entertain rather than to inform the public because sensationalism sells newspapers and television ads. To this end, the media attempts to build excitement around a "horse race" between the candidates, thus avoiding the discussion of the complexity of the campaign issues.

By nature, "gate keeping" follows a "trickle down" process. The media selects topics or parts of topics to cover which create images that play on and direct people's emotions. The desired image trickles down to the public creating anxieties or making people feel good about a candidate or issue. In 1992, this type of media demagoguery or "gate keeping" occurred when the media chose to emphasize the fact that Bush renounced his no new tax policy, but failed to discuss the merits of what he was trying to accomplish and the impact on the economy that a $66 billion increase* in the deficit had caused. Thus, the gate keeping process in the 1992 election helped create electoral choices by making

*In 1988 the deficit was $155.2 billion and by 1990 it was $221.2 billion.

Clinton appear to be a more politically attractive choice than Bush, who was portrayed as untrustworthy and out of touch with the people and the economy. In a January, 1996, interview, Hugh Sidey a Contributing Editor from Time magazine in Washington, D.C., acknowledged the magazine treated Clinton very well and Bush unfairly during the 1992 election. Instead of questioning the merit and validity of Bush's action, the media focused on his character. Bush felt the media's "gate keeping" contributed greatly to his defeat in 1992 and shifted the emphasis away from what he, many members of Congress, and the public felt were the most serious problems facing the nation – the deficit and the national debt.* Rather, the media was more interested in an issue of character and a catchy sound bite. The real issue was fiscal policy and in what direction the country should be moving – something the media missed altogether.

B. The Role of Presidential Leadership

Students of the Presidency commonly divide the institution's development into two major periods: **traditional** and **modern.** The traditional Presidency is associated with those Presidents who conceived of their role as the **chief administrative** head of the federal government but **not** as a **legislative leader or policy maker.** The transition from the traditional to the modern Presidency, in a political sense, began during the Presidency of Andrew Jackson. As the forerunner to modern Presidents, Jackson became a strong President by asserting his leadership in public policy over the legislative and judicial branches. Jackson asserted that the President's right to judge the constitutionality of legislation was no less than that of the Supreme Court and in 1832 he dared Chief Justice John Marshall to enforce his ruling in *Worcester v. Georgia.* Jackson succeeded in these defiant actions because his Presidential authority was supported by his popularity among his constituency.

Jackson was ahead of his time. His leadership style laid a foundation for the transformation of political power in the Presidency

---

*The national debt is the sum of the nation's past deficits and is currently about $5 trillion.

that would emerge in the formation of the modern Presidency. It was not until the Progressive Movement (1901-1917), during the Presidencies of Theodore Roosevelt and Woodrow Wilson, that the concept of the modern President as the popular and legislative leader reappeared. The Progressives, who tried to correct the most serious economic and social faults which accompanied the growth of big business in the post-Civil War period, wanted a President who would lead Congress in a national crusade. The Progressive spirit created the support for Theodore Roosevelt who, like Jackson, believed the President possessed a special mandate from the people: he was "a steward of the people bound actively and affirmatively to do all he could for the people. . . ." Theodore Roosevelt expanded upon Jackson's model of leadership by joining popular leadership to a greater sense of national purpose – a "new nationalism" that foretold of an unprecedented expansion of the government's responsibility to secure the social and economic welfare of the nation.

In an economic and social sense, then, the modern Presidency also has its beginnings with Theodore Roosevelt and Woodrow Wilson during the Progressive Movement. The idea of the federal government regulating any aspect of society was new and not fully accepted within society. Consequently, with America's involvement in W.W. I, in 1917, the Progressive Movement and the idea of federal regulation of society was temporally lost. However, the Progressive Movement laid the philosophic and some of the legislative foundations for the New Deal. With the Great Depression of the 1930's and the leadership of Franklin D. Roosevelt came the final acceptance by the public of government regulation of society. Not only did the public expect the government to regulate the economy to provide economic and social stability as a result of the Depression and FDR's leadership, but they also demanded it.

Presidents before the Progressive Movement, and following the Progressive Movement, up to Franklin D. Roosevelt, were not concerned about the condition of the economy. These traditional Presidents were only involved with microeconomic policy, a term used to describe government regulation of specific economic activities, e.g. deregulation of trade. Traditional Presidents did not regard the overall management of the economy as a primary policy responsibility. An example of microeconomic policy in which a traditional President showed little concern for the management of the country's economic well-being is found in the Panic of 1837. President Martin Van Buren supported the Independent Treasury system that required all government specie to be removed from private banks and placed in various sub-treasuries around the country. Tariff revenues and receipts from land sales were also deposited in these storage centers and government expenditures were made in cash. Van Buren's Independent Treasury system reflected what little regard he had for the nation's economy. By removing all federal funds from private banks, Van Buren removed federal funds from the state economies, which reduced the state's supply of investment capital, thereby contributing to the growing economic recession. Van Buren's actions with the Independent Treasury **reflected his narrow image of the Presidency** as simply a protectorate of federal funds and not as a national social or economic leader. Van Buren argued that the funds should be withdrawn from private banks so that, "the fiscal operations of the United States be placed on such a basis that they may be embarrassed as little as possible by the doings of banks and speculators." Hence, the historical pattern before Roosevelt was that most Presidents did little more than ride out the storm.

As a modern President, Franklin Roosevelt, when confronted by enormous domestic and international crises during the 1930's, began a program of action and innovation involving macroeconomics unmatched by any chief executive in our history. During his first 100 days in office, the nation witnessed a President whose social and economic revolution has become the yardstick against which the performance of his successors is measured. Consequently, the public now expects the President to control business cycles through macroeconomic policy – management of the entire economy.

In carrying out macroeconomic policy there are two principal tools: **fiscal policy** and **monetary policy.** Fiscal policy refers to the government's discretionary efforts to regulate the level of the nation's economic activity either by seeking to expand the economy by increasing spending and reducing taxes, or to contract it by decreasing spending and increasing taxes. Monetary policy refers to the government's efforts, through the Federal Reserve System, to regulate economic activity by controlling the supply of money, thereby influencing interest rates, credit, and the conditions of credit.

In controlling business cycles through public policy, there are historically three goals of macroeconomic policy that drive Presidential action which have remained constant since the Presidency of FDR: (1) To establish and maintain maximum employment, (2) to achieve a steady rate of **real** economic growth, and (3) to maintain purchasing power by price stability with control over the rate of inflation or deflation.

The general public's attitude that the government, and in particular the President, is responsible for their welfare and the well-being of the economy was initiated by Congress' legislative actions and Roosevelt's active leadership role as chief of state during the Great Depression. After Roosevelt's death, Congress reinforced the idea that the President is responsible for the state of the economy by passing the Employment Act of 1946. Theoretically, the statute committed the United States government to a macroeconomic policy to maintain "maximum employment, production, and purchasing power." Yet, the act did not require the government to maintain full employment nor set goals it must meet, and it furnished the President with few new resources to achieve its stated goals. However, the Employment Act did require that, (1) a Council of Economic Advisers and an accompanying staff be created and (2) the President report annually to Congress on the condition of the economy with proposals for improving or maintaining its health. Yet, the ultimate power over the President's macroeconomic proposals remained with Congress and it still does. The President was only given the power to suggest legislation. Congressional approval remains a Constitutional requirement.

In fact, since 1974 Congress has had the means to create its own macroeconomic package and is able to require the President to carry out its programs by forcing him to spend all funds appropriated. The political environment created by the Vietnam War and Watergate Era caused Congress to assert greater authority over the Presidency. A product of this congressional hostility was the passage of the *Congressional Budget and Impoundment Control Act of 1974,* often referred to as the Congressional Budget Act (CBA).

The CBA instituted a new process which enabled Congress to establish overall congressional policy goals by allowing members to react to the budget as a whole rather than in pieces as it arrived from the various appropriation committees. Congress still receives the President's budget in January and still takes testimony from administration officials. During the summer months the old authorization appropriations process still takes place. Congress takes testimony from executive agency officials and considers the President's budget on individual spending bills in the separate appropriation committees. The difference is that Congress now better understands the overall budget process because it has its congressional committees armed with information that now allows them to develop their own budget and policy guidelines independent of the President's.

On May 15 of each year, the first congressional budget resolution is supposed to be enacted. The resolution sets targets for budget authority and outlays, spending by functional category, revenues, surplus or deficit, and public debt. By September 15 of each year, Congress is required to pass the second budget resolution, which sets binding totals. Those figures must be reconciled with the actions of the appropriations committees in time for the start of the new fiscal year — October 1.

In order to enable Congress to create its own budget document, the CBA created the Congressional Budget Office (CBO). The CBO helped dissolve the "budget resources gap" between the two branches by providing Congress with its own source of information independent of the President or Executive branch. Consequently, Congress no longer depends on the economic assumptions and budget projections provided to them by the Office of Management and Budget (OMB) in the executive branch. Thus, in the creation of the budget, a major power shift occurred between the President and Congress when Congress gained access to budget information provided independently of Presidential influence. This process significantly reduced the influence of the President and substantially increased the influence of Congress over the budget.

Another way the CBA enhanced Congressional budgetary influence was by imposing new congressional controls on the President's ability to control funds that have been budgeted. Historically, Presidents have impounded funds that have been budgeted, trying to save federal money on programs they felt were unnecessary. The CBA limited Presidential power in the budgetary process by creating a procedure whereby the President can only request that Congress temporarily delay spending (deferral) or permanently eliminate spending (rescission). Deferrals automatically go into effect unless either house disapproves of them within forty-five days. Rescissions are automatically rejected unless both houses approve of them within forty-five days. If the President refuses to abide by congressional disapproval of impoundments, the act further authorizes the Comptroller General to initiate legal action in the federal courts to force compliance with the will of Congress. The Constitution is silent on whether the President **must** spend the money that Congress appropriates; all it says is that the President cannot spend money that Congress has not appropriated. Since 1803 many Presidents have taken advantage of this constitutional ambiguity to impound appropriated funds they believed unnecessary or wasteful. In 1803, Thomas Jefferson deferred a $50,000 appropriation for gunboats. Ulysses Grant returned to the Treasury unspent money for public works. In 1932, Herbert Hoover canceled projects funded by Congress. Franklin D. Roosevelt deferred spending on a number of appropriations to later fiscal years. Harry Truman did not spend all of the money that Congress had allocated for the military, nor did Lyndon Johnson spend the money allocated for highway construction and John Kennedy did not spend 7.8 percent of the budget in 1961.

The question of whether the President is required to spend all appropriated funds came to a head in 1972 during the Nixon administration after a number of confrontations over this issue between the President and an antagonistic, Democratic-controlled Congress. When Nixon vetoed appropriation bills, Congress often overrode his vetoes. After Congress overrode a Presidential veto to pass the 1972 Clean Water Act, Nixon impounded $8.7 billion of the $18 billion that was intended to implement the act. In addition, during a news conference on January 31, 1973, President Nixon asserted that the constitutional right of a President to impound funds for the purpose of combating inflation or avoiding a tax increase was "absolutely clear."

Although officials in the Nixon administration invoked the Jefferson incident as an acceptable precedent, Jefferson's action was temporary and provoked by changing events. Nixon's announcement and actions broke new constitutional ground; consequently, cities, states, and certain members of Congress sued the Nixon administration over its refusal to spend appropriated funds. Federal courts handed down approximately eighty decisions that ruled on the impoundment theories; the Nixon administration lost all but three of those. One case, *Train v. City of New York* (1975) reached the Supreme Court. The Court ruled unanimously that the President had to spend money appropriated by Congress because of his obligation to "take care that the laws be faithfully executed." Presidents may no longer defer funds simply because they do not support the policies enacted into law by Congress.

Ironically, in 1981 the Reagan administration was able to use the CBA as an executive tool. Reagan used the 1974 budget process to push his fiscal program of increased defense spending, decreased domestic spending, and a large tax cut through Congress. The CBA's centralized budget-making process in Congress allowed him to negotiate with congressional leaders on the substance of his entire budget plan rather than being forced to bargain on a dozen or more appropriations bills, each of which might have been opposed by a different congressional bloc. To get his budget approved, Reagan used his public popularity to build a conservative coalition in the House of Representatives despite the Democratic majority. The new budget process allowed all the cuts to be packaged into a single bill; hence, members could announce that they objected to specific cuts but could support the bill "on balance."

Another point regarding limitations on Presidential macro-economic policy is the **Structural Budget Deficit Problem (SBDP)**. The foundation for this SBDP was laid during FDR's administration with the passage of the Social Security Act in 1935. In 1960 the U.S. Census Bureau data indicated that 22 percent of Americans had incomes below the poverty line. Thus, during the 1960's, in an effort to use the wealth generated by the economy to promote social welfare and care for the less fortunate, decisions were made to create and enlarge public programs called entitlements.* The creation and expansion of entitlement programs, along with the automatic cost-of-living adjustments that were tied into the programs and **structurally** built into the budget during the early 1970's, allowed spending in these areas to grow faster than the rate of the economy and made the struggle to limit budget deficits almost impossible by the 1980's. Structurally building in the cost-of-living adjustments is a classical example of good politics but bad governance. In 1963 entitlements accounted for 22.6 percent of the budget. By fiscal year 1983, entitlements had risen to 45.2 percent of the budget; consequently, Congress believed additional budget reform was necessary to control spending. Although several budget control measures were discussed, including a line-item veto for the President and a constitutional amendment to balance the budget, a strategy of mandatory spending cuts was the alternative chosen by Congress, and in 1985 Congress passed the Gramm-Rudman-Hollings Act (GRH).

The GRH represented a major revision in the budgetary process by providing for a multi-year deficit reduction timetable

---

*Entitlements are provided for in federal law as a legal right to payments from the U.S. Treasury. Entitlements include Social Security, Medicare, Medicaid, unemployment compensation, farm subsidies, Supplemental Security Income, food stamps, public assistance, and federal retirement.

for bringing the federal budget into balance. By imposing declining deficit ceilings, it would bring the budget into balance by 1991. If the deficit exceeded the guidelines, the GRH provided for automatic enforcement through across-the-board cuts on discretionary spending, or sequestration. The premise was that the threat of massive spending cuts required to bring the budget into balance would force the President and Congress to negotiate timely and prudent agreements to reduce the deficits. However, questionable budget accounting and political practices postponed the deficit crisis until 1990 when the deficit was more than double the GRH maximum, making compliance to the GRH impossible. In summary, the failure to reduce entitlement spending levels during the 1980's effectively precluded substantial reductions in the deficit. Also, the national debt that emerged from the Reagan era (it tripled from 994.8 billion in 1981 to 2,868 billion in 1989) limited the flexibility of Bush to conduct economic stabilization policies. The Bush administration had inherited an economic and political time-bomb encompassed in the structural budget deficit problem and the GRH. Bush could not contemplate an economic policy response to recession without first considering what such a response might do to the deficit and interest rates. To complicate matters, the political dispute, over the level and composition of spending and tax policy necessary to balance the budget was not just between Democrats and Republicans, but among Republicans themselves. Since history has shown a strong connection between economic conditions and reelection, Bush had a powerful incentive, as a first term President, to attempt to create short-term economic success. In looking for the right way to create economic recovery, Bush knew any long-term economic plan required a strategy to lower the deficit. By 1990, the country needed leadership based on good governance and not party politics, which both President Bush and Democratic House Speaker Thomas Foley were willing to provide. The extent of this leadership will be discussed under the budget agreement.

C. Sources of Presidential Power

The power of the Presidency is derived from six sources: (1) the Constitution, (2) the expansion and contraction of Presidential power by congressional action or inaction, (3) the expansion of Presidential power by custom and practice, (4) the expansion of Presidential power by institutional change, (5) the expansion of Presidential influence by the force of historical events, and (6) the expansion from the President's personal capacity to influence public opinion and government officials.

I. The Constitution: Article II, Sections 1, 2 and 3 establishes five areas of Presidential power as (1) chief of state, (2) chief administrator, (3) chief legislator, (4) commander in chief, (5) and chief diplomat. Article 1, Section 7, also helps establish the President's power as chief legislator.

Chief Administrator. As chief administrator, the President is manager of the nation. This role of the President is limited by the Constitution, by acts of Congress, and his image of the Presidency. This power is more implied than defined in the Constitution. Article II, Section 1, simply states: "The executive Power shall be vested in a President of the United States of America." Article II, Section 3, says only that "he shall take care that laws be faithfully executed." Acts of Congress are more specific about the role of the President in implementing the law. Though historically Congress has expanded Presidential power and responsibility, acts of Congress can and do limit Presidential power, e.g. the Congressional Budget Act of 1974.

Additionally, Presidential leadership is somewhat illusionary because the executive branch consists of **separated institutions sharing power.** Executive agency administrators are responsible to the President, but they are also responsible to Congress, to their staffs, their clients and to themselves. Their personal attachment to the President is all too often overwhelmed by their duty to other masters. This point is best illustrated by a statement from FDR's Secretary of State, Cordell Hull:

Half of a President's suggestions, which theoretically carry the weight of orders, can be safely forgotten by a Cabinet member. And if the President asks about a suggestion a second time, he can be told that it is being investigated. If he asks a third time, a wise Cabinet officer will give him at least part of what he suggests. But only occasionally, except about the most important matters, do Presidents ever get around to asking three times.

The definition of chief administrator is continued under Sections 2 and 3 of Article II. Section 2 states: "he may require the opinion, in writing, of the principal officer in each of the executive departments, upon any subject relating to the duties of their respective Offices. . . ." Section 3 states: "He shall from time to time give to the Congress information of the State of the Union, and recommend to their Consideration such Measures as he shall judge necessary and expedient; he may, on extraordinary Occasions, convene both Houses, or either of them, and in Case of Disagreement between then, with Respect to the Time of adjournment, he may adjourn them to such Time as he shall think proper. . . ." As the federal government has grown, so has the significance of these powers. What all of this means is that the President has the duty and the power to give information and make recommendations to Congress, but he does not have the power to enforce those recommendations.

Chief Legislator. Besides contributing to the President's role as chief administrator, Section 3 of Article II also contributes to his role as chief legislator: "He shall from time to time give to the Congress Information of the State of the Union," and to recommend such other measures for its consideration as deemed "necessary and expedient." Two critical factors of modern Presidential leadership rooted in this section are legislative agenda setting and program development. These factors were not fully accepted until the development of the New Deal by FDR. It is now expected of the President as head of the national government to exercise a compelling vision by initiating programs to promote the economic and social well-being of the American people. Today a President is expected to develop a congressional coalition to carry out, support, and pass his programs and communicate his **vision** of these programs effectively to the public.

The President's role as chief legislator is also established Constitutionally by his veto power in Article I Section 7:

> Every Bill which shall have passed the House of Representatives and the Senate, shall, before it becomes a Law, be presented to the President of the United States; If he approves he shall sign it, but if not he shall return it, with his Objections to the House in which it shall have originated, who shall enter the Objections at large on their Journal, and proceed to reconsider it. If after such Reconsideration two-thirds of that House shall agree to pass the Bill, it shall be sent together with the Objections, to the other House, by which it shall likewise be reconsidered, and if approved by two thirds of that House, it shall become a Law. If any Bill shall not be returned by the President within ten Days (Sundays excepted) after it shall have been presented to him, the Same shall be a Law, in like Manner as if he had signed it, unless the Congress by their Adjournment prevent its Return in which Case it shall not be a Law.

During an era of divided government (when one party controls the Presidency and the other controls Congress) the veto power of the President becomes a key means of leadership and control. By 1995 there had been a total of 2,524 Presidential vetoes and only 105 overrides by Congress.

The effect of the veto power on public policy is both negative and positive. It is negative by nature; once used, it signifies an impasse between the President and Congress, and policy is unchanged as Congress has refused to go along with the President's ideas and he has refused to accept its idea. Sometimes a President finds that the veto is the most effective means of communicating his intentions to Congress. President Gerald Ford's sixty-eight vetoes, for example, were his way of conveying his social and economic policy preferences to a liberal Democratic Congress. The positive aspect of the veto lies in its use as a bargaining tool to shape, alter, or deter legislation. By threatening to exercise the veto – a threat made credible only by actual use – the President can define the limits of his willingness to compromise with Congress. He can state in advance what he will and will not accept, thereby reducing the likelihood of a showdown over a bill. Selective and sensitive use of the threat to veto can be a means of avoiding or of reconciling conflict with Congress. For example, in his first two years, President Bush frequently threatened to veto bills as a way to stimulate serious bargaining. By not making empty threats and picking them carefully, Bush managed to avoid overrides. In fact, his 98 percent success rate (only one of forty-four vetoes was overridden) is unprecedented for a President with a Congress controlled by the opposition party.

Chief of State. Every nation has at least one person who is the ceremonial head of state. These leaders embody the spirit of the nation and symbolize the nation to their people and the world. The British have a King or Queen; the Japanese have an Emperor. In the United States the President as chief administrator is head of the government and by tradition is ceremonial chief of state. Under Article II, Section 3, he is also responsible to "receive Ambassadors and other public Ministers." It is in this capacity as chief of state that a President has the greatest opportunity to expand his Presidential power by use of his personal influence. Sarah McClendon, a White House correspondent for eleven Presidents from FDR to Bill Clinton, stated it well, in a recent interview, when she said the most important leadership quality a President can possess is being a people person: acting as head cheerleader, radiating confidence, and encouraging the masses. Hence, when a national crisis like the depression of the 1930's happens, the greatest benefit to the American people offered by a President like FDR is emotional leadership and support that gives them hope for the future and faith in themselves and the country.

In his capacity as chief of state, the President engages in a number of activities that are largely symbolic or ceremonial. The most dramatic involves consoling the people after natural disasters such as hurricanes and floods or terrorists' acts such as the Oklahoma City bombing of 1996. Other ceremonial activities include receiving visiting chiefs of state, going on official state visits to other countries, and making personal telephone calls to congratulate the country's heroes and greeting them at the White House.

Commander in Chief. According to Article II, Section 2, the President is "commander in chief of the army and navy of the United States, and of the militia of the several States, when called into the actual service of the United States." At the same time Article I, Section 8, gives Congress the power "to declare war." Thus, the President may conduct war by commanding the troops, but only Congress has the power to declare war. It is this **sharing of power** (not only with war making duties, but with all Presidential duties) that comprises the system of checks and balances that has fueled most of the constitutional conflict between Congress and the President.

In addition to the extant record of the proceedings of the Constitutional Convention and writings of the Founding Fathers, such as the Federalist Papers, history also serves to indicate the intent of the Constitution's framers. Numerous historical examples demonstrate that an official declaration of war by Congress is not necessary nor always desirable for a President to **make war** or engage in military activities. It is the President who decides when an armed conflict is a war; once the President has defined a military operation as an armed conflict and not a war, and Congress does not take action to contravene his interpretation, the President's decision may stand. One of many historical examples that could be used to demonstrate this point can be found during John Adams' Presidency in 1798 when Adams involved the United States in an undeclared naval war with France. The war was the result of the XYZ Affair in 1798, when Adams felt it necessary to protect the integrity of the United States government and the lives and property of American citizens. Adams' actions were opposed by Vice President Thomas Jefferson, leader of the opposition party, and his fellow Republican party members in Congress. Although Congress did not officially declare war, it passed twenty different legislative measures between March 27 and July 16, 1798, providing for the consolidation of the national defense. During the XYZ Affair, a declaration of war would have been detrimental to the U.S. national interest. England was at war with France at that time. A declaration of war could have been perceived by France as an alliance with England and could have complicated an attempted peace settlement with France. As it was, the undeclared war was enough of a threat to France to make her want to settle her differences with the United States.

As Adams' Vice President, Jefferson opposed Adams' military action as a result of the XYZ Affair. Once Jefferson became President, his views on the use of Presidential power changed. As President, in 1801, Jefferson involved the United States in an undeclared war without the consent of Congress with the Tripolitan pirates. Jefferson dispatched war craft to the Mediterranean and then notified Congress after the ships had left. Congress did not object to Jefferson's, actions but passed legislation authorizing the arming of merchant ships in order to defend American interests in the war. By so doing, Congress helped establish the precedent that a formal declaration of war was not necessary prior to an armed conflict initiated by the President and that subsequent actions of Congress, supporting the President's actions, would suffice to meet the constitutional requirement. Jefferson's actions with the Tripolitan pirates along with John Adams' actions during the XYZ Affair, established this early precedent. This precedent has also been confirmed by subsequent events which have involved the United States in over 200 military operations with only five declarations of war from Congress: the War of 1812, the War with Mexico between 1846-1848, the Spanish American War, World War I, and World War II.

There is little debate about the President's power to manage armed conflict once war has been declared. There are, however, a number of constitutional questions about what constitutes a war, who can involve the United States in armed conflict, and (if the United States is not under attack) under what circumstances the President can commence hostilities. In its attempt to constrain the war-making power of the President and reacting to the unhappy experience in Vietnam, Congress enacted the War Powers Resolution in 1973. The War Powers Resolution requires that the President:

> In every possible instance (the President) shall consult with Congress before introducing United States Armed Forces into hostilities or into situations where imminent involvement in hostilities is clearly indicated by the circumstances and after every such introduction shall consult regularly with the Congress until United States Armed Forces are no longer engaged in hostilities or have been removed from such situations.

The Resolution goes on to state: "Within sixty calendar days after a report is submitted or is required to be submitted. . . the President shall terminate any use of the United States Armed Forces. . . ." unless authority is extended by Congress. Since the passage of the War Powers Resolution, a number of questions have arisen about the extent of the President's war-making powers without congressional involvement.

The questions raised by the War Powers Resolution will remain political questions, for while the Constitution assigns legislative power to Congress and executive power to the President, the Constitution does not sharply define the separation between them. To the contrary, the Constitution builds in numerous points of contact and overlapping power, thereby creating an invitation to conflict between the two branches. Although the War Powers

Resolution does not change the Constitutional relationship between the branches of government, each political crisis that calls
forth a military solution forces the President, Congress, and the
American people to evaluate the nature of the conflict and the appropriate response to a greater extent than otherwise might be the
case. Thus, historically, the War Powers Resolution has contracted
the President's power as commander in chief. It has created a political cloud over his Constitutional powers, but at the same time
it might force a President to act more cautiously, thereby supple-
menting the check and balance process.

Chief Diplomat. The President's power to make war com-
bined with his power to make treaties "by and with the Advice and
Consent of the Senate," makes him the country's chief diplomat.
His role as chief diplomat also stems from his power to "receive
Ambassadors and other public Ministers" as well as to nominate
ambassadors with the approval of the Senate.

Presidents have varied in how closely they collaborated with
the Senate in making treaties, most waiting until after negotiations have been concluded before allowing any Senate participation. More significantly, the conduct of foreign affairs has come to
rely on executive agreements between heads of state in place of
treaties. Executive agreements are international agreements entered into by the President without reference to treaty or statutory
authority; that is, they are made exclusively on the basis of the
President's constitutional powers as chief executive and commander in chief. These agreements are not subject to Senate approval and in international law they are as effective as formal
treaties in conferring rights and obligations. Modern Presidents
are more apt to make executive agreements than treaties. By 1994
United States Presidents had agreed to 14,392 executive agreements compared to only 1,482 treaties. The majority of these executive agreements (13,210) have been negotiated since 1939,
while only 683 treaties have been ratified during this same period.

With the Constitutional authority "to receive ambassadors,"
Presidents have discovered an independent power beyond the

reach of Congress. This power is the ability to unilaterally set the course of foreign policy by recognizing the independence of countries without the consent of Congress. For example, recognition of the Soviet Union by Franklin Roosevelt in 1933 was a momentous decision; likewise, Nixon's recognition of the People's Republic of China in 1972 was of equal significance. Presidents have not always taken this responsibility upon themselves. In the 1830's when the matter of recognition of an independent Texas posed a vital policy question, President Andrew Jackson believed the decision was best left to Congress. Abraham Lincoln followed this same policy in regards to recognition of Haiti and Liberia. Hence, modern Presidents have expanded their power and influence in foreign policy by exercising their power to recognize the independence of countries, while traditional Presidents have deferred to Congress.

II. Congressional Expansion of the Presidential Power: The greatest extension of Presidential power over congressional power derives not from the President's unbounded self-serving interpretation of his inherent authority, but from the power extended to him by Congress and the Supreme Court. Congress often extends the President's power by legislating an increase in executive authority. At other times, the President's power is expanded by the lack of congressional reaction to his actions and subsequent approval from the Supreme Court. It is this interaction of Congress and the President that ultimately defines the scope of powers of both branches. One example of congressional expansion of Presidential power was already discussed above in section I with the actions of the President as commander in chief.

Another example of congressional expansion of Presidential power deals with the use of executive agreements during Theodore Roosevelt's Presidency. Although the first executive agreement identified by historians was authorized by Congress in 1792 establishing the first post office and required a postal agreement with the British colonies in Canada, it was not until Roosevelt's presidency that executive agreements became widely used. In 1904 the financial affairs of the Dominican Republic were in a desperate state; consequently, the Dominican Minister appealed to Roosevelt "to establish some kind of protectorate" over the island and save it from its European creditors. In 1905 Roosevelt entered into an agreement (the Dillingham-Sanchez Protocal) with the Dominican Republic to establish an American financial protectorate over the island. When the Senate was unwilling to support his agreement, Roosevelt responded by implementing the Dominican protectorate through an executive agreement. Two years after the executive agreement was in place, the Senate finally acquiesced and approved the treaty with minor modification.

In 1936 the Supreme Court provided a foundation for upholding executive agreements as domestic law in the case of *United States v. Curtiss-Wright Export Corporation.* This decision thus gave a ringing endorsement of independent Presidential authority in the area of foreign affairs. As the United States acquired global responsibilities, engaged in nuclear diplomacy, fought undeclared wars, and debated the requirements of internal security, the *Curtiss-Wright* case gave proponents of an expanded Presidential role a constitutional foundation.

A final foreign policy example of congressional action that expanded Presidential power is the passage of the National Security Acts of 1947 and 1949. These acts centralized the military aspects of defense planning and operations under the secretary of defense, who is directly responsible to the President. Thus the President was charged with the task of coordinating national security policy – foreign policy, intelligence collection and evaluation, and defense policy.

Congressional expansion of power in domestic affairs for the modern President developed as Congress legislated responsibilities that earlier Presidents chose to avoid. The traditional Presidents' lack of interest in being the economic managers of the country has already been demonstrated with the example of Martin Van Buren's action during the Panic of 1837. Congress has since expanded the modern Presidents' fiscal responsibilities and potential power with the creation of the Bureau of the Budget in 1921 (within the Department of the Treasury) and the passage of the Employment Act of 1946 which requires the President to become the nation's **economic manager.** Since 1921, one of the most important powers delegated by Congress to the Presidency has been the formulation of the budget of the United States and its submission to Congress, a process that involves both symbolism and substance. The budget is a plan for the nation's finances, and therefore represents a statement of national priorities. As such, it dictates how much money goes to defense and domestic needs, if taxes should be raised or lowered, and whether there will be a balanced budget, a deficit, or a surplus. The budget provides an opportunity to influence the nation's economy, to adjust taxing and spending, to spur growth, or to restrain inflation. Symbolically, the budget reflects the modern Presidents' values and leadership abilities, whether in proposing bold new spending initiatives, offering sweeping tax cuts, or resolving to reduce the budget deficit as Bush did during the 1990 budget negotiations with Congress. Today, budget policy remains one of the most critical challenges of the American Presidency.

III. Expansion of Presidential Power by Custom and Practice: The expansion of Presidential power by custom and practice includes the practice of (1) the President acting as his party's leader and (2) the President responding to national events that create social and economic crises.

The origin and development of American political parties stands entirely apart from the Constitution. In fact, almost all of the framers despised the idea of "factions." In the Constitution they tried to create a government that would discourage the formation of national parties. The framers of the Constitution knew that conflict among organized groups was bound to occur as it had occurred during the drafting of the document itself. Such divisions in society were bound to lead to factions, which would struggle to gain control over state and federal governments. The framers feared these struggles would bring out people's worst failings: selfishness, ambition, and deceit. In order to gain the advantage, political parties and their leaders might stop at nothing.

From the beginning, George Washington's conduct as President reflected his understanding of the Presidency as a nonpartisan office. Like most of the framers of the Constitution, he disapproved of factions and did not regard himself as the leader of any political party. However, Washington's conception of the nonpartisan Presidency did not survive even his own administration. Party conflict arose from the sharp differences between Hamilton and Jefferson, differences that began during Washington's first term and became irreconcilable during the second term. The end of Washington's administration marked the transformation of the Presidency from a nonpartisan to a partisan institution. Thereafter, Presidents might try to rise above the party, but partisanship had become a critical ingredient of Presidential leadership in order to defend their actions and carry out their public policy.

Theodore Roosevelt expanded the power of the Presidency and established the practice of a President interceding in a national economic crisis during the Anthracite Coal Strike of 1902. Roosevelt used the Presidency as an agent to guarantee a "just balance", or a Square Deal as he called it, between rival groups in society. Roosevelt became the first President in history to recognize the rights of labor in an industrial dispute.

The strike began when the United Mine Workers, under president John Mitchell, struck on May 12, 1902, for higher wages, union recognition, and an eight-hour day. Rather than follow the example of Cleveland, who sent troops to break up the Pullman strike of 1894, Roosevelt called representatives of the coal industry and the miners to the White House, asking both sides to agree to a new contract in the interest of the health and welfare of the nation.

When the coal industry balked at Roosevelt's proposal, he was prepared to take more drastic action. If Roosevelt could not persuade labor and management to accept arbitration voluntarily, he threatened to appoint a settlement board without their consent and arrange for the governor of Pennsylvania to request federal assistance to keep the peace and order. Roosevelt also intended to have federal troops "seize the mines and run them as a receiver for the government." Nowhere was the President's right to seize and operate private property even hinted at in the Constitution, much less specified. Without legal precedent or congressional legislation to justify his involvement, Roosevelt moved the government away from its traditional position of isolation from such internal economic and social struggles.

The Anthracite Coal Strike is only one example of Roosevelt's public policy which introduced the concept that the modern President and the national government are responsible to the people for the social and economic welfare of the nation. His leadership expanded the role, power, and expectation of Presidential leadership in the minds of the public during the time of the Progressive Movement.

IV. Expansion of Presidential Power by Institutional Change: The time and complexity involved in managing the executive branch today cannot compare with the Presidency of John Adams or Andrew Jackson. Adams had the top of his desk divided into fourteen compartments 4" by 5", by which he organized the business of the whole executive branch, while Jackson, like all of his predecessors before him, personally signed every land grant issued to the general public by the federal government. It was during Jackson's Presidency that Congress created the first departmental clerk who was authorized to do no more than sign land grants. Before 1857 the President was not even allowed a private secretary paid for with public funds. Today, the Presidency is a complex institution where the President appoints more than 2,000 full-time assistants in the White House and in the specialized units of the Executive Office.

The Executive Office of the President (EOP), created in 1939, houses the President's personal staff, policy experts, and the President's cabinet. The White House Office staff consists of 500 to 600 personal assistants to the President, including his close personal advisers, press agents, legislative and group liaison aides, and special assistants for domestic and international policy. They help the President maintain communication with Congress, the executive agencies, and the public. They work in the White House and are hired and fired by the President.

The President is also served by the policy experts in different offices in the EOP who are not located in the White House. These offices employ economists, legal analysts, national security specialists, and others. Some of the more important offices include the Office of Management and Budget (OMB), the office of Policy Development, the Council of Economic Advisers (CEA), the Central Intelligence Agency (CIA), and the Office of Personnel Management (OPM).

Fourteen federal agency heads, by tradition, constitute the President's cabinet. Some Presidents have relied on the counsel of their cabinets while others have solicited the opinions of their cabinets and then done what they wanted to do anyway. Lincoln supposedly said – after a cabinet meeting in which a vote was seven nays against his one aye – "Seven nays and one aye; the ayes have it." During the Bush administration, within the fourteen agencies alone there were about 2,000,000 civilians employed in cabinet departments. In contrast, in 1800 the total federal bureaucracy consisted of 3,000 civilian employees, more than a third of whom were employed in mail delivery.

The federal government, and therefore, the President's management responsibilities have increased with the growth of population, geography, and the economy. Also, the United States' increased role in world politics has expanded not only our own expectations, but that of other countries around the world. Consequently, it is not simply the complexity of the office that has changed, but also the depth and vastness of the problems that one man is expected to understand and address.

V. Expansion of Presidential Power by the Force of Historical Events. Historical events have created circumstances or opportunities for Presidents to expand their influence. The Civil War, the Progressive Movement, and the Great Depression are a few classic examples that allowed Presidents Abraham Lincoln, Theodore Roosevelt, and Franklin D. Roosevelt the opportunity to accomplish great deeds and demonstrate strong leadership. Each period of Presidential dominance in American history has been marked by a special set of circumstances such as a war or a compelling national problem that convinced Congress and the public that bold Presidential action was needed. Thus, great Presidential leadership has come about not as a result of Presidents creating the historical events, but as a result of their actions taken during these times of crisis. All of the Presidents that have been rated by historians as great (Lincoln, F. Roosevelt, Washington, and Jefferson) or near great Presidents (T. Roosevelt, Wilson, Jackson, and Truman) have been "crisis Presidents." Because Presidential power used during these events has been so awesome, it has created unrealistic images and expectations by the public of the office holder. The problem for most Presidents is that without a crisis, conditions are not normally conducive to strong Presidential leadership because the dominant public opinion supports the status quo. Also, some Presidents are "transitional Presidents" and contribute to the process of change by serving in periods when important problems are surfacing, but have not yet become critical or their solutions obvious. In many cases "transitional Presidents" are one term Presidents or are only viewed by historians and the public as average or above average Presidents. In the area of civil rights, John F. Kennedy is an example of a "transitional President." Kennedy recognized that federal intervention would be necessary to bring social justice to black Americans, but was unable to convince Congress of this before his assassination. Kennedy's assassination on November 22, 1963, was an extraordinary event. No other incident, with the possible exception of the assassination of

President Lincoln in 1865, can match its impact on the public. The fact that it played instantly on television helped produce enormous public grief. Johnson, who was deeply committed to civil rights himself, resolved to continue the work begun under Kennedy and to make the passage of a civil rights bill a monument to his memory. Thus, Johnson became the "crisis President," able to seize the moment by profoundly changing American race relations when he gained passage of the *Civil Rights Act of 1964.*

VI. Expansion of Presidential Power by use of Personal Power. A President must always remember that an important source of Presidential power is his personal and political reputation because an essential ingredient for effective Presidential leadership is the ability and/or willingness of a President to create public support for his public policies. A President must have the ability to see emerging historical patterns and problems, while simultaneously, have the ability to communicate those problems and their solutions effectively to Congress and the general public.

In Washington power means influence, and a President's personal power stands on his capacity to influence the opinion of the general public and the conduct of congressional leaders. A President's ability to provide guidance in the policy-making process and to enlist congressional support for his programs depends on his willingness and ability to lobby Congress, his rhetorical abilities, and the political skill of his staff. Many members of Congress and some members of President Bush's staff felt that the lack of political skill by some of his key staff members to lobby Congress, as well as Bush's own unwillingness to communicate the deficit problem and solution as he saw it to Congress and the general public were major reasons for the defeat of his first 1990 budget agreement.

Theodore Roosevelt was the first of the modern Presidents to develop the rhetorical Presidency, which expanded the President's ability to guide the formation of public policy by becoming the leader of public opinion. Roosevelt was an eloquent speaker, and is said to have been the first to describe the Presidency as a "bully pulpit," He was the first President to use popular rhetoric as a principal technique of Presidential leadership. The rise of the rhetorical Presidency signified a dramatic transformation from the early history of the Presidency. The framers of the Constitution had envisioned the Presidency as an administrative branch. Thus, during the nineteenth century, direct Presidential efforts to rouse public opinion in support of policy initiatives were considered illegitimate, a form of demagoguery beneath the dignity of the office. Roosevelt's "stewardship" theory of the executive, however, demanded that a stronger popular connection be forged. Accordingly, Roosevelt appealed directly to the people to bring pressure to bear on members of Congress reluctant to support his policies. His ability to enact a considerable portion of his public policy in spite of the tepid support, and even the obstructive resistance from members of his own party, indicated that a new era of Presidential leadership had arrived.

Another great rhetorical President, Franklin D. Roosevelt, made such a great impression on the American political system that in the most recent survey of historians, he was ranked as the second greatest President in history, surpassed only by Abraham Lincoln. Above all, FDR's high ranking is owed to his efforts to lead the American people through the Great Depression. Roosevelt came to office in the fourth year of a world economic crisis. The persistence of the economic crisis not only created dissatisfaction with business leadership in America, but led to a crisis in confidence with the system of Western capitalism, democracy, and most significantly how the American people perceived themselves. One of the keys to understanding the significance of Roosevelt and the New Deal is understanding this crisis in confidence.

In mid-March of 1933, Roosevelt held Congress in session and launched a program that led to fifteen major laws in a hectic 100 days. From the first, Congress and various pressure groups shaped the New Deal's political and economic contours, leading critics to charge that it was not a coherent plan and would not work. And in fact, based on its economic success, the New Deal, was only partially successful. However, based upon its use of optimistic psychology, the New Deal was a great success in dealing with the crisis in confidence. Roosevelt acted as head cheerleader, radiating confidence, and skillfully using his office to explain his **creative vision*** to the American people that the New Deal was the hope for the future. FDR's ability to deal with this crisis in confidence made him the yardstick by which contemporary Presidents are judged. He did this with his legislative leadership during that first 100 days of his administration and by transplanting his **vision** for the country into the hearts and minds of the American people. Roosevelt's rhetorical skills used during his thirty-one fireside chats was one of the key tools used to transplant this vision.

Another President whose personal power rested on his rhetorical skill to communicate his ideology to the American people was Ronald Reagan. Although Reagan won by a landslide in the electoral college, sweeping forty-four states with 489 electoral votes, he received only 51 percent of the popular vote. Reagan's ability to transform his ambiguous electoral victory into concrete legislative achievements testifies to his considerable personal skills at wooing both the public and members of Congress. Critics dismissed his ability to communicate effectively as a former actor's trick of the trade – namely, to learn and deliver his lines. But Reagan's supporters maintained that there was logic and substance to his message, that he was not simply the "Great Communicator" but the "Great Rhetorician" who, like Woodrow Wilson and the two Roosevelts before him, articulated a **creative vision** that inspired the nation. The Republican Contract with America and the 1994 Congressional elections demonstrate that Reagan's words and political **vision** continue to stir deeply rooted and widely shared American political values. Reagan's enormous popular appeal was based on the simplicity of his message, the dignity of his public demeanor, and the fact that he demonstrated a strong sense of direction backed by the strength of his convictions.

---

*Defined as the ability of a President to articulate a policy that captures the public's imagination and convince the public that country is moving in the right direction, regardless of the success or failure of the policy.

Besides the FDR and Reagan leadership model, another model needs to be understood: the Lincoln, Ford and Bush model of **good governance** versus successful party politics. What is often overlooked in times of crisis is the political courage that lead to a conscious choice between successful political policy and good governance, oftentimes coming at the expense of personal political success. A political axiom by presidential scholar Richard Neustadt illustrates this political problem: "a President must always consider the effect of his decisions on his prospects for the successful exercise of presidential power in the future." Although Neustadt's axiom is true, a President must protect his personal power and effectiveness, or he may become a lame duck earlier than he thinks if Congress and the public view him as inept. However, the needs of the country sometimes require that a President have **flexible vision*** to see beyond his personal views and the political courage to challenge the beliefs of those members of his own party, members of Congress, and the general public as to the correct direction the country should take. At these times Neustadt should be ignored.

The historical lesson, whether one is a Lincoln, a Ford, an FDR, or a George Bush, is that there are some political and economic problems that only time can solve regardless of political rhetoric or legislative leadership skills. An essential ingredient of public leadership is to have the ability to define the policy dilemmas facing the nation in terms of an emerging historical situation. Only great leaders may have the vision to see the emerging historical situation and the **flexible vision** and political courage to exercise **good governance** by adjusting their personal and/or political values to what is in the best interest of the country. Even though this vision might lead in an unpopular direction with political consequence, it must be followed. What is important is not the success or failure of one man, but the future of this nation and the world. Our

---

*Flexible vision involves the ability of a President to see problems as they develop along with the ability to change or adjust his views when his views are no longer in the best interest of the public or congruent with the changing political, social or economic situation. Flexible vision does not include the ability to create a vision in the minds of the public.

Founding Fathers felt that power was to be used by men of conscience, vision, and integrity for the common good. Therefore, power is a trust and public office an opportunity for public service. Thus, the challenge for President Bush in 1990 was (1) would he have the flexible vision to see and understand the emerging deficit problem, (2) would he have the political courage to use his opportunity for public office to put the best interest of the country above his own personal or political needs, and (3) would he be able to articulate the emerging deficit problem and his solution to the public in a way that would capture their imagination and convince them that he was moving in the right direction.

CHAPTER II

DEMONSTRATING
PRESIDENTIAL LEADERSHIP

To demonstrate the different aspects of political pragmatism and to put the model of good governance versus good politics into historical perspective, the actions of three past Presidents (Thomas Jefferson, Abraham Lincoln, and Gerald Ford) will be discussed. The actions of these Presidents in times of crisis demonstrate five key points about Presidential leadership: (1) a President's political reversals on public policy must be looked at in context of their benefit to public policy; (2) a President's tough decisions are often unappreciated during his Presidency by the public and can lead to a one term Presidency; (3) a President must have the vision or ability to see the direction in which the country must move; (4) a President must have the political courage to make tough decisions and adhere to his decisions regardless of the personal or political consequences, and (5) a President must be prepared for the political reality that both his foreign and domestic policies, regardless of their merits, will be attacked by the opposition party even when the attack requires a reversal of the opposition party's previously advocated positions.

THOMAS JEFFERSON

A. Thomas Jefferson

From a leadership perspective, Thomas Jefferson's Presidency is important because it reflects Jefferson's ability to adjust his strong sectional and personal philosophy for the benefit of the nation. Jefferson's Presidency helps demonstrate that in times of crisis a President may need to make a conscious choice to reverse his own political actions or beliefs for what he believes is vital to the national interest. Such actions as Jefferson's or Bush's should be evaluated on their merit and their relationship to the national interest and not on previous actions or statements. Jefferson's leadership helped to cultivate programs in the public interest that transcended party lines and helped build a national identity. Before his Presidency, Jefferson, like many of the Republicans of his time, viewed himself more as a citizen of Virginia than as a citizen of the United States. As such, he was a states' rights advocate and a strict constructionalist of the Constitution. However, during his Presidency, when he was forced to deal with challenges from foreign countries, Jefferson became a loose constructionalist, thus proving to be a strong nationalist. As his actions related to the Louisiana Purchase demonstrate, his **"political pragmatism"** was an essential ingredient of effective Presidential leadership which helped the states evolve into a nation in reality and not just in name. Before Jefferson's actions related to the Louisiana Purchase can be articulated and appreciated, a brief history of the origins of political parties and their ideologies must be understood.

The first national parties developed from sectional opposition in Congress in the early 1790s as a result of Secretary of the Treasury Alexander Hamilton's financial program. James Madison and Jefferson, both Southerners from Virginia who saw Hamilton's program as running contrary to the agricultural interests of the South, organized opposition to Hamilton and his program. Northern congressmen in the House of Representatives supported the bill that created Hamilton's Bank of the United States in 1791 by a margin of thirty three to one, while Southern representatives opposed it nineteen to six. As their antagonism to Hamilton endured, and as the widely read newspapers of the day took sides, spreading their political messages, primitive semblances of political parties emerged. Hence, by 1792, the foundation for America's political party system was established as a result of the bitter clashes between Hamilton, Jefferson, and Madison over fiscal policy as well as foreign affairs.

By 1793-1794, these sectional factions and distinct ideological identities had acquired names – Federalists, representing Hamilton's views and finding broad support in the North, and Democratic-Republicans, representing the views of both Jefferson and Madison and finding broad support in the South. The ideological differences of the two parties extended beyond the Bank of the United States. In domestic policy, Republicans believed in a strict interpretation of the Constitution which would limit the powers of the federal government to those powers enumerated in the Constitution. This meant that any increase in federal powers would require a Constitutional amendment. In contrast, in domestic policy the Federalists believed in a loose interpretation of the Constitution that would enhance the power of the federal government. In political and social philosophy, Republicans believed in government run by the wealthy who would rule in the interests of the common man, while the Federalists believed the government should be run by the wealthy for the interests of the wealthy. In economic philosophy, the Republicans supported the interests of agriculture, whose popular support was strongest in the South and in the back country, and the Federalists supported business and commercial interests, whose popular support was strongest in New England and along the Atlantic sea coast. Finally, in foreign policy, Republicans were pro-French and anti-British, while the Federalists were pro-British and anti-French.

During this period the political struggle between the British and French dominated world politics and profoundly affected the outcome of the American Revolutionary War. France proved herself to be America's strongest ally. French support during the Revolutionary War and Jefferson's attachment to the ideas of the French enlightenment caused Jefferson and his party to be decidedly pro-French in sentiment. However, the economic relations that many colonists, particularly in the northeastern colonies, had developed with England during their colonial period were still highly desirable after the war. Consequently, after the War for Independence, the North was predominately pro-British, while the South and many of its leaders (like Jefferson) were pro-French.

The problems which led to the Louisiana Purchase started during Jefferson's Presidency in October, 1800, when Napoleon (France) secured from Spain in a secret treaty (San Idefonso) the territory of Louisiana. Rumors of this transfer between France and Spain were partially confirmed in October, 1802, when the Spanish, who still controlled the territory for the French, canceled the right of deposit. The right for American traders to deposit their cargo at New Orleans was given to the United States under the Pinckney Treaty in 1795. Losing this right meant goods shipped by American traders initiated in the Mississippi and Ohio Valleys would not be allowed to be transferred to ocean-going vessels at the port of New Orleans. This serious disruption of American commerce made it impossible for Western farmers to get their produce to market. This posed not only a serious economic threat, but a political one as well.

The political problem developed as a roar of anger rolled up and down the Mississippi and Ohio Valleys as many Westerners talked of descending upon New Orleans with rifles in hand if Jefferson and the United States government failed to protect their commercial rights. To avoid conflict with the French and to keep the support of the Westerners, Jefferson instructed Robert Livingston, the United States minister in Paris, to purchase the port of New Orleans for $2 million.

In January, 1803, Jefferson asked James Monroe to join Livingston in Paris and offer up to $10 million for New Orleans and the Floridas. By the time Monroe joined Livingston, Napoleon had lost interest in establishing an American empire and offered to sell the entire Louisiana Territory for $15 million. Napoleon's desire to create an empire in the Americas had faded when the French lost the island of Santo Domingo due to military resistance and yellow fever. The threat of a new war against Britain in Europe prevented France from sending reinforcements, and Napoleon now feared a possible invasion of Louisiana by American settlers or loss of the area to the British if and when war broke out in Europe. Napoleon was also influenced by threats made by Jefferson of a possible war with the United States.

Jefferson demonstrated his **political pragmatism** by going against his personal pro-French feelings when he warned Napoleon, "The day that France takes possession of New Orleans, we must marry ourselves to the British fleet and nation." The action of France, Jefferson wrote, "completely reverses all the political relations of the United States, and will form a new epoch in our political course. . . ." The President continued, "It is New Orleans, through which the produce of three-eighths of our territory must pass to market, and from its fertility it will ere long yield more than half of our whole produce and contain more than half of our inhabitants." Consequently, by a treaty and two conventions, all dated April 30, 1803, the negotiations were completed. Thirteen states would eventually be carved out of the acquisition that doubled the land area of the United States by adding some 828,000 square miles between the Mississippi River and the Rocky Mountains. The agreements provided that $15 million would be paid: $11,250,000 for the territory and $3,750,000 to settle past claims by American ship owners against France.

Although the Mississippi River and the Gulf of Mexico were set as the eastern and southern boundaries of the purchase, neither Livingston nor Monroe were certain how much land they had actually purchased because the other boundaries were not defined, leaving the status of West Florida and Texas unclear. When they asked Talleyrand, the French foreign minister, whether the deal included Florida, he responded ambiguously, "You have made a noble bargain for yourselves, and I suppose you will make the most of it." Even at that moment, Livingston realized that the transaction would alter the course of American history. "From this day on the United States take their place among the powers of first rank."

Nevertheless, certain difficulties about the "noble bargain" remained. The French Constitution prohibited the disposal of territory without a legislative vote, a step with which Napoleon had dispensed. The American Constitution, in turn, did not explicitly delegate power to purchase foreign territory to the President or any other department or branch of government. Had Jefferson continued his political and philosophical advocacy of a strict interpretation of the Constitution, he would have lost the "noble bargain." Jefferson felt an amendment to the Constitution would have taken too long because the window of opportunity that Napoleon had offered could be lost with changing political conditions in Europe; thus, the territory was purchased by way of a treaty even though the right to do so was not explicitly stated in the Constitution. In October, 1803, the Senate approved the treaty twenty four to seven and the House appropriated the purchase money ninety to twenty five. And on December 20, 1803, the United States formally took possession of Louisiana. The Louisiana Purchase illustrates that there are times when a President must, for the sake of the national interest, contradict his previous personal beliefs and political philosophy. Jefferson justified his reversal in Constitutional philosophy with the following statement:

> A strict observance to the written laws is doubtless one of the high duties of a good citizen, but it is not the highest. The **laws of necessity,** of self-preservation, of **saving our country when in danger,** are of a higher obligation.

From an historical perspective, Jefferson's actions seem well justified and are an example of good governance and public policy that should have gone unquestioned by the opposition party – the Federalists. However, **politics required** the Federalists to change their **public advocacy** and interpretation of the Constitution from a loose constructionalist to a strict interpretation. The Federalists argued the Republicans had no constitutional basis for the transfer of land. What they really feared were the **political conse-quences** of the signing of the Louisiana treaty. The signing of the treaty could be their own political death warrant since new states would be carved from the new territory that would outvote the thirteen charter states including Federalists New England. The Federalists knew it was likely these new states would philosophi-cally support and vote along the same pro-agriculture lines as Jef-ferson's Republican party and against the commercial interests of the Federalists in New England.

The parallel to President Bush in 1992 to the 1803 election is that **politics required** the Democrats attack Bush for his 1990 budget agreement as a reversal of his 1988 campaign pledge not to raise taxes. The political attack came even though the Democ-ratic leadership in Congress worked together with Bush on the 1990 budget agreement to increase taxes. Then, three years later, the Democratic Congress worked with President Bill Clinton to produce the 1993 budget agreement. This latter agreement in-cluded $496 billion in budget cuts and a $177 billion tax increase, $40 billion higher than Bush's 1990 budget. The Democrats' change of their public advocacy on taxes was good short-term pol-itics because it helped contribute to Clinton's victory in the 1992 election. However, for the Democratic members of Congress, the political attack on Bush's tax policy proved in the 1994 congres-sional elections to be bad long term politics. Just as the Federalists (during the process of the Louisiana Purchase) changed their in-terpretive view of the Constitution as it applied to public policy for **political reasons,** so, too, did the Democrats, under the lead-ership of President Clinton. The problem with this process was that the Democratic party, between 1990-1992, put their politi-cal interest above the interest of the country, just as the Federalist party had done in 1803. Because the American people understood neither the deficit issue nor Bush's actions, and because they took Clinton and the Democrats at their word in 1992, they felt be-trayed by the Democrats' 1993 budget agreement. A Bush quote from his State of the Union Address on January 28, 1992, *(See Chapter IV, Page 195)* puts this parallel into political perspective:

> I understand that politics is, for some, a game – and that sometimes the game is to stop all progress and then decry the lack of improvement. . . . When people put their party's fortunes – whatever the party, whatever side of the aisle – before the public good, they court defeat not only for their country, but for themselves.

The 1994 congressional election proved Bush's insights to be correct as the public gave the Democratic party one of its worst defeats in congressional history.

In conclusion, political parties modify their public policy as it suits their political needs as demonstrated by the Federalists in 1803 and the Democrats between 1990-1993, but political reversals must be looked at in the context of their benefit to public policy. When political leaders like Jefferson or Bush make political reversals on public policy, what is important is the motivation behind the reversal and its purpose. In the cases of Jefferson or Bush, the greater duty to the national interest as they saw it was the driving force, and not personal or political gain. A personal letter to President Bush from President Richard Nixon dated June 29, 1990, illustrates this point:

> You are taking heat on the tax issue, but you had no choice but to do exactly what you did. . . . As you know, I had to burn a lot of my own speeches and eat a lot of words when I went to China in 1972. What mattered most was not that I had changed my mind, but that I had done what I thought was best for the country and for the cause of peace in the world.

Finally, Jefferson's new interpretation of the Constitution helped create a movement away from Americans feeling they were more citizens of a particular state than they were of the United States. By helping the states evolve into a nation not just in name, but in reality, Jefferson contributed to the development of a strong federal government which had the power to act in the best interests of the people. In foreign policy, Jefferson's purchase of Louisiana proved to be a landmark decision. Overnight, he avoided a possible rupture with France, while at the same time avoiding an entangling alliance with England and allowed the nation to continue the noninterventionist policies of the Federalists before him. The historical lesson demonstrated by Jefferson's action was that political pragmatism proved to be an essential ingredient for realizing the national interest.

ABRAHAM LINCOLN

B. ABRAHAM LINCOLN

Abraham Lincoln is our greatest Presidential pragmatist. Lincoln's pragmatism has raised some interesting and controversial Constitutional questions which will not be debated here, but only discussed to illustrate his use of political pragmatism. The question that needs to be asked is what made Lincoln great? Part of the answer to that question was Lincoln's (1) ability to see the "greater goal" or the direction the country must move, (2) his willingness to make the tough and unpopular decisions, and (3) the courage with which he adhered to those decisions regardless of the personal or political consequences.

The actions of great leaders are not always appreciated by their contemporaries, as Lincoln's pragmatic attempts to preserve the Union demonstrate. In fact, members of Lincoln's own party rejoiced at the news of his death and the accession of Andrew Johnson to the Presidency. A quote from Congressman George Julian, R-In., is representative of these feelings:

> I spent most of the afternoon in a political caucus and while everybody was shocked at his murder the feeling was nearly universal that the accession of Johnson to the Presidency would prove a godsend to the country. Aside from Mr. Lincoln's known policy of tenderness to the Rebels...his...views of the subject of Reconstruction were as distasteful as possible to radical Republicans.

What this quote reflects is that during many historical crises, society does not have the vision to recognize effective Presidential leadership, and that only time will allow that appreciation to develop. This point has already been demonstrated with the results of Bush's 1990 budget agreement and the revitalized economy the agreement created. The point is further demonstrated by the Presidential rankings of both Lincoln and Truman. Lincoln is now rated our greatest President and Harry Truman who left office with a popular rating of 32 percent is now rated by scholars as a "near great" President. The reasons for this change appears to be two fold: (1) the American people are too close to a problem as it develops within society and lack an historical perceptive to evaluate the problem and (2) the American people fall prey to the demagoguery of the political process and the media and lose sight of the real issues. What all this means, is that the **first lesson** of leadership demonstrated by Lincoln is that a President must have the **courage of his convictions.** If a President falls prey to the political pressures within society and compromises himself or what he believes to be right in his conscience, then he has failed himself, the office of the Presidency, and most important of all, he has failed the people who elected him to **use his judgement** to represent their interests – even if they disagree with his judgment. The following quote from the British statesman, Edmund Burke, was often used by President Bush to illustrate this point:

> It ought to be the happiness and glory of a representative to live in the strictest union, the closest correspondence and the most unreserved communication with his constituents. Their wishes ought to have great weight with him; their opinions his highest respect . . . . But his unbiased opinion, his mature judgment, his enlightened conscience – these he ought never sacrifice to you. . . . Your representative owes you not only his industry, but his judgment; and he betrays, instead of serving you, if he sacrifices it to your opinion.

To understand the value and significance of Lincoln's leadership, a brief explanation of the causes of the Civil War is necessary.

The pump was primed for the Civil War as a result of the war with Mexico between 1846-1847, which lead to the acquisition of California and the Southwestern portion of the United States in 1848 (Treaty of Guadalupe-Hidalgo). The acquisition of this territory posed a question which Americans of the next decade could not evade. Would it be the destiny of the United States to spread slavery or freedom?

John C. Calhoun and Ralph Waldo Emerson had little else in common, but both men sensed in the Mexican War the omens of a great disaster. Calhoun warned that Mexico was "the forbidden fruit; the penalty of eating it would be to subject our institutions to political death." "The United States will conquer Mexico," Emerson conceded, "but it will be as the man swallows the arsenic. . . . Mexico will poison us." Wars, as both men knew, have a way of breeding new wars, often in unforeseen ways. Hence, the winning of the Southwest gave rise to quarrels over newly acquired lands. The debate over the expansion of slavery became the "key issue" during the late 1840s and throughout the 1850s. In each case the quarrels set in motion a series of disputes which continued to pull at the emotional, psychological, and political seams of the country until it exploded into civil war.

By 1860 a political environment had been created which made it impossible for anyone to avoid a civil war; however, this did not stop Lincoln from trying. During his inaugural address he expressed a willingness not only to support a constitutional convention to solve sectional issues, but also to endorse a proposed amendment "to the effect that the federal government, shall never interfere with the domestic institutions of the States, including that of persons held to service."

Once war began, Lincoln was at first less willing than ever to interfere with slavery, for his assessment of population and geography led him to believe that the secession of the border slave states, even Kentucky alone, might make the South an unconquerable power. As the war progressed, Lincoln's willingness to deal with the slavery issue changed as the political environment changed both overseas as well as at home. The **second lesson** of leadership represented by Lincoln's actions comes from the **flexibility in his attitude** towards slavery. The significance of this flexibility is that it is done for the purpose of keeping the greater goal in sight and not as a tool for personal or political profit. This flexible attitude becomes apparent in the following open letter from Lincoln to Horace Greeley in a New York newspaper:

My paramount object in this struggle is to save the Union, and is not either to save or destroy slavery. If I could save the Union without freeing any slave, I would do it; and if I could save it by freeing some and leaving others alone, I would also do that. What I do about slavery and the colored race, I do because I believe it helps to save the Union: and what I forbear, I forbear because I do not believe it would help to save the Union. I shall do less whenever I shall believe what I am doing hurts the cause, and I shall do more whenever I shall believe doing more will help the cause.

I shall try to correct errors when shown to be errors, and I shall adopt new views so fast as they shall appear to be true views.

To Lincoln, any measure necessary to bring a successful conclusion to the war was worth taking. Once a person becomes President, the burden of upholding the integrity of the office of the Presidency also causes its occupant to reflect on events differently. Bush, like Lincoln, had a flexible mind. Great leaders have **flexible minds** and flexible vision. Herein lies Lincoln's greatness. He was willing to do anything to prevent the war, but once it started, he would take any measure to bring it to a speedy conclusion, even if it meant freeing no slaves. Lincoln, as the following quote illustrates, realized that there are times when unpleasant means are justified in order to accomplish the greater goal – of preserving the Union.

My oath to preserve the Constitution to the best of my ability imposed on me the duty of preserving, by every indispensable means, that government – that nation, of which the Constitution was the organic law. Was it possible to lose the nation and yet preserve the Constitution? By general law, life and limb must be protected, yet often a limb must be amputated to save a life; but a life is never wisely given to protect a limb. I felt that measures otherwise unconstitutional might become lawful by becoming indispensable to the preservation of the Constitution through the preserving of the nation. Right or wrong, I assume this ground, and now avow it.

As the War progressed, Lincoln saw that the slavery issue could be used to help accomplish the greater goal of preserving the Union by defining the war as democracy's struggle for survival, which he plainly came to believe himself. Lincoln's **third lesson** of leadership derives from the **vision he had to see the correct path** the nation must take towards this greater goal. At the same time, he had the willingness and ability to cultivate this policy, even when it challenged party lines, his own personal beliefs, and threatened his physical and political well being.

In order to preserve the Union, Lincoln understood the necessity of enabling his countrymen to believe they were embarked on an ennobling crusade. As he stated:

> It presents to the whole family of man the question whether a constitutional republic, or a democracy – a government of the people, by the same people – can or cannot maintain its territorial integrity against its domestic foes. It presents the question whether discontented individuals, few in number, can arbitrarily break up their government and thus practically put an end to free government upon the face of the earth.

While Lincoln was defining the war as democracy's struggle for survival, other men around him wanted a different, more radical definition. For them, slavery was the issue. Thus, the Emancipation Proclamation was a political by-product in Lincoln's attempt to "save the Union."

Not only was the Emancipation Proclamation an effective political tool at home, but also overseas. The South claimed it was fighting the war as its only hope against Northern economic aggression to preserve its life style, as well as political aggression to preserve the sovereignty of the various states. Even though England and France had been critical of the United States' practice of slavery, the Southern views about Northern economic and political aggression were gaining support in both countries because England and France would have liked to have seen the United States' political power weakened in the western hemisphere. This, along with their need for Southern cotton, created the possibility of both countries entering the war on the side of the South. Lincoln's vision gave him the ability to see the necessity of changing the official goals of the war from preserving the Union to abolishing slavery by use of the Emancipation Proclamation.

The executive leadership of Lincoln during the War embodied the broadest interpretations of Presidential authority under the Constitution up to that era. As commander in chief, he called up seventy-five thousand Union volunteers to defeat what he defined as an insurrection by rebellious individuals. His initial actions after the Confederate attack on Fort Sumter included calling Congress into extraordinary session, but he set a date eighty days after his call for the convening of the members. He also ledged a large monetary sum to pay for the military buildup and suspended the writ of habeas corpus in several regions, all without the prior authorization of Congress.

This successful assertion of executive authority by Lincoln was initially made in a Congressional vacuum because some members had chosen to support the Confederacy while many others had left Washington, D.C., to return to their states or districts. Since the Constitution specifically granted Congress the power to declare war, raise and support armies, and maintain a navy, Lincoln's decisive actions in these and related areas were unprecedented. Like the Congress, the Supreme Court was sharply divided over the constitutionality of Lincoln's sweeping actions, but in the *Prize Cases* (1863) the Court narrowly upheld Lincoln's blockade of the Confederacy and, indirectly, all the earlier actions he authorized. The Court reasoned that when confronted by war, the President was obliged to take all appropriate actions "without waiting for any special legislative authority." Thus, with Congress' lack of action and the Court's decision in the *Prize Case*, Presidential power had been expanded and confirmed within an historically practiced political process.

The powers that Lincoln was willing to assert as commander in chief during the Civil War freed him to use the executive office energetically and to deal with the problem of preserving the Union. Part of the significance of the Emancipation Proclamation was that it was a political tool used by Lincoln to "save the Union" as his open letter to Horace Greeley in the New York newspaper indicates. Because the Emancipation Proclamation was based solely upon the war powers given the President in the Constitution, the Proclamation's authority to free slaves was limited to areas under military occupation. The Emancipation Proclamation also initiated an irreversible revolution in race relations. This revolution led to the Thirteenth Amendment (the granting of freedom or the abolishment slavery), the Amendment Fourteenth (the granting of citizenship to black Americans, "due process," and "equal protection under the law") and the Fifteenth Amendment (the granting of the right to vote to black Americans) to the Constitution, plus additional civil rights legislation from 1866 to the present.

A clear illustration of political pragmatism as was used by both Jefferson and Lincoln is demonstrated by the following quote from President Richard Nixon. In it, Nixon comments on this balanced use of political power and idealism that is needed to have the vision to be a great leader.

> There are times when unpleasant means are justified in the service of a great goal. But despite the protests of the process-lovers, a proper means never justifies an unsatisfactory end. No matter how democratic and meticulously correct it may be, a political process that cannot produce progress for a nation has gone seriously awry.

There is no magic in democracy. The Constitution, extraordinary document that it is, cannot by itself produce a moment of peace or an instant of prosperity. Only the will and the vision of leaders, exercised through the democratic system, sometimes restrained by it, occasionally even exceeding it, can bring about these goals. Idealism without pragmatism is impotent. Pragmatism without idealism is meaningless. The key to effective leadership is pragmatic idealism.

The historical lesson learned is that a President must do whatever it takes to protect and preserve policies and goals that are vital to the national interest whether it meant acquiring the Louisiana Territory, fighting a civil war, or dealing with a financial crisis that is mortgaging the future of our children. A President must try to carry out his public policies as his judgement or conscience dictates. Even if his efforts fail, he has succeeded because he has done what he believed was in the best interest of the nation and what was in his heart. History has recorded Lincoln's pragmatic actions as examples of great leadership. Bush's actions in reference to the 1990 budget agreement demonstrate the same principles of leadership: (1) a vision of the "greater goal" and the direction the nation must move, (2) the willingness to go in that direction regardless of previous commitments, and (3) the courage to continue in that direction regardless of the personal or political consequences.

GERALD FORD

Gerald R. Ford

– Photo courtesy Gerald R. Ford

C. Gerald R. Ford

George Bush and Gerald Ford have more in common than the office of the Presidency. Both Presidents made leadership decisions that each believes contributed significantly to his electoral defeat. Each had the courage to follow his conscience and act in the country's best interest knowing there would be a political price to pay. Finally, both Presidents are examples of the Presidential model of leadership that leads to one-term Presidents. First-term Presidents must weigh, in times of significant conflict, their perception of the national interest against the cost of reelection — good governance versus good politics. Presidents who choose good governance and act counter to public opinion do so because they believe the public has lost sight of what is in its best interests as a result of the media's demagoguery and the intentional distortion of the issues by the opposition party. Both Presidents Bush and Ford found themselves participating in this type of decision making process. Both Presidents chose the best interest of their country over what would be good politics for themselves. This process of choosing good governance over good politics has led to many one-term Presidents from John Adams and the XYZ Affair to George Bush and the 1990 Budget Agreement. However, choosing his country's needs over personal or political needs does not make a President a political failure; on the contrary, it makes him a successful leader and a model of Presidential leadership that needs to be recognized and appreciated by the public.

A final example of political pragmatism as effective Presidential leadership is Ford's act of pardoning Richard Nixon on August 9, 1974. Ford's controversial decision to pardon Nixon was based on his vision that the country, fragmented by Watergate and its political repercussions, needed "a time to heal." The key ingredients to understanding Ford's motives and how they led to his decision are "balance" and "reality." Ford had to "balance" the economic, political and social needs of the country with the "reality" of what **could** be done with Richard Nixon and what **should** be done.

Ford's final decision to pardon Nixon became a matter of conscience and thus a self-evident truth to Ford as he made clear in his speech when pardoning Nixon: "The Constitution is the supreme law of our land and it governs our actions as citizens. Only the laws of God, which govern our consciences, are superior to it." Ford, like Bush, followed Edmund Burke's law that stated: "Your representative owes you not only his industry, but his judgment, and he betrays, instead of serving you, if he sacrifices it to your opinion." Ford, thus also adhered to Lincoln's first lesson of leadership: the courage to follow his convictions.

No single motive was the force behind Ford's pardon of Richard Nixon. Ford's vision of a fragmented America and his reflections about the emotional, economic, political, personal, and interpersonal relations that surrounded Nixon, the country, and himself are intertwined with the following five factors which formed the bases for his decision:

(1) The primary factor was his inability to deal adequately with the nation's economic problems and foreign policy issues with the Nixon distraction hanging over his head.

On October 17, 1974, in his testimony to the House Judiciary Subcommittee, Ford stated that part of his decision for the pardon was based on the impact the trial would have on the country. Ford estimated that 30 percent of his time was spent in dealing with Nixon related matters, slowing down the decision making process for both domestic and foreign policy issues. In Murphy v. Ford a federal district court agreed with Ford's actions and stated:

> In view of the fact that public clamor over a former President's alleged misdeeds in office had not immediately subsided on his resignation and that at the same time the country was in the grips of an apparently uncontrollable inflationary spiral and an energy crisis of unprecedented proportions, it was not unreasonable for the successor to the office to conclude that the public interest required that positive steps be taken to end the division caused by the scandal and to shift the focus of attention to the more

pressing social and economic problems; thus, by pardoning the former President, the successor was acting in accord with the letter and spirit of his constitutional power to grant pardons, since he was taking steps to restore the tranquillity of the commonwealth by a well-timed offer of pardon.

(2) The next concern for Ford was Nixon's health. Closely associated with this concern was Ford's feeling of compassion and sympathy for Nixon, and Ford's strong personal desire to show him mercy.

Nixon's mental and emotional state at the time was difficult to judge and is still the subject of conflicting assessments. Even though Ford stated that compassion for Nixon as an individual had not prompted his decision, his actions, past statements, and statements from his former aides conflict with such a statement. For example, on the morning of September 8 when Ford informed Tip O'Neill that he was pardoning Nixon, one of the responses Ford gave to O'Neill's question of "Why?" was, "Nixon is a sick man. And Julie has been calling me every day because her father is so depressed." When Phil Buchen, a member of Ford's staff, was asked by reporters why Ford had not demanded a confession of guilt from Nixon as a condition of the pardon, Buchen replied, "You do not put conditions on an act of mercy." Buchen and other members of Ford's staff still argue today that the pardon was an act of mercy, and the health of Nixon and his family were strong considerations for Ford in issuing the pardon.

(3) The third problem that troubled Ford was Nixon's ability to get a quick and fair trial and the degree of punishment needed to achieve justice. The Nixon pardon created an illusion for the American people that Richard Nixon slipped away without being punished, and therefore was above the law. The questions are did he, and what constitutes "just punishment"?

Ford's conclusion was that justice brought about through a court room would not be justice in "reality" for either the American people or Nixon. Ford recognized the age old problem of theory versus reality and that they seldom match. In this case, Ford made his decision arguing that punishment had been meted out to Nixon by the way he left office and justice could not be better served by prosecuting him. Hugh Sidey of Time describes in a very graphic way how Ford came to this realization on August 8, after he was summoned to the White House for a meeting.

> What occurred to Ford in a way that even he has a hard time defining was the final realization of the horrible price that Nixon was paying for his guilt, which everybody, including Nixon, knew that he was carrying. The notion that Nixon was cynically slipping beyond punishment was just not true. Ford, sitting beside Nixon's desk, perceived it in a dimension no one else could see or feel.

In viewing Nixon's pain and humiliation as a result of his resignation from the Presidency, Ford saw the reality of the issue of justice and its utility for the American people. What purpose should punishment serve and who should be exempt from traditional punishment? Ford's answer was that punishment should fit the crime. Since Watergate was viewed by Ford (and Nixon himself) as a **political crime,** Nixon's resignation from the Presidency was the harshest of all punishments. In his book, Man of the House, Tip O'Neill seems to agree when he remarks, "After all, it's not where a man lands that marks his punishment. It's how far he falls." Because Nixon's forced resignation was not a traditional punishment, it was not considered a harsh punishment by the majority of the American people, but the factors of, **balance, reality, and the needs of the country** must be kept in mind in dealing with the punishment of a President, any President.

(4) Ford's next concern was the emotional distraction created by the press over the issues surrounding Nixon, his own impatience with the Nixon related problems, and his strong desire to put these problems behind him. If the pardon had not been

granted, Ford would have had to answer questions constantly about Nixon and be prepared at all times to deal with a problem he did not want and did not have the mental energy to confront.

At his first press conference on August 28, Ford naively thought the press corps' primary interests would be in the economy and changes in the White House staff and foreign affairs, such as Cyprus or the SALT talks. He was wrong. Ford became frustrated because the press was not interested in him or how he planned to deal with the substantive issues of the economy or foreign affairs. Rather, the press continued to be obsessed with Nixon. When he asked his aides how long they felt this would go on, they replied that it would continue as long as Nixon's legal status and the disposition of his papers and tapes remained unclarified. After his August 28 press conference, Ford realized, "I'd be questioned repeatedly about him and his many legal problems. . . I had to get the monkey off my back. All this forced me to address the issue squarely for the first time."

(5) The final factor in Ford's decision to pardon Nixon was concern for the political and emotional problems of the country, his political party, and for his own political future. In expressing his concern about the potential problems for the country in his testimony before the House Judiciary Subcommittee, Ford stated that shortly after the August 28 press conference:

> I became greatly concerned that if Mr. Nixon's prosecution and trial were prolonged, (estimates were from one to two years) the passions generated over a long period of time would seriously disrupt the healing of our country from the wounds of the past.

To say that the dominant reason Ford pardoned Nixon was to help the party or himself in the upcoming November elections or in 1976 is an oversimplification of the problem. However, to say that it was not a part of the motive would be incorrect as well.

Politically, Ford **(but not the country)** would have been better off letting the matter go through the impeachment process. The downside with the impeachment process was that it would have consumed a great deal of his as well as Congress' time, and thus any chance of solving the problems of the economy would have been minimized. The declining economy greatly reduced Ford's chances of being elected; however, by granting the pardon, he destroyed any chance. For many Americans, the granting of the pardon destroyed the great affection they had had for Ford, and it established in their eyes the idea that he could not be trusted because he had been tainted by Nixon.

In evaluating Ford's character and political past practice of always saying and doing what his conscience told him was right, it is doubtful that any deal would have been made in an effort to clear the way for his election two and one-half years later. For Ford, the choice was good governance versus good politics – either choice was a disaster. For the country, however, there was only one right answer, and Ford chose it.

Tip O'Neill, a former Speaker of the House and a Democrat, but also a loyal friend of Ford's, perhaps overstated Ford's virtues, but spoke honestly when he said, "God has been good to America, especially during difficult times. At the time of the Civil War, he gave us Abraham Lincoln. And at the time of Watergate, he gave us Gerald Ford. . . ." These were indeed the right men at the right times who helped us survive the two greatest political crises our country has faced. The transition from Nixon's administration to Ford's was done with stability and respectability, and thus showed the greatness of our Founding Fathers in designing a system that could make such a smooth transition. For the most part, one would have to say that the pardon served the best interests of the country and that Ford (despite what one thinks of Nixon) showed political courage and leadership abilities when pardoning Nixon.

For Ford or any President including Jefferson, Lincoln, or Bush, it is not what their critics say or do that counts, but it is what these men have accomplished or attempted for the public interest that counts. Whether they failed or not, their pragmatic efforts were and are essential ingredients of effective leadership.

The feebleness of the criticism of those who have criticized Presidents for following their own consciences and entering into the arena to accomplish the "greater goal" for the good of the nation is illustrated by a quote from Theodore Roosevelt.

> It is not the critic who counts; not the man who points out how the strong man stumbles, or where the doer of deeds could have done them better. The credit belongs to the man who is actually in the arena, whose face is marred by dust and sweat and blood; who strives valiantly; who errs, and comes short again and again; because there is not effort without error and shortcoming; but who does actually strive to do the deeds; who knows the great enthusiasms, the great devotions; who spends himself in a worthy cause, who at the best knows in the end the triumphs of high achievement and who at the worst, if he fails, at least fails while daring greatly, so that his place shall never be with those cold and timid souls who know neither victory nor defeat.

There will always be critics of the Presidents' actions as Ford's pardoning of Nixon, Jefferson's Louisiana Purchase, and Lincoln's actions to preserve the Union have demonstrated, but there must always be a person in the White House who has the vision to see the greater goal and the willingness to lead the country in that direction regardless of the political or personal consequence for himself. A President must be willing to give up the Office of the Presidency for something that he believes in; he should care more about the country than he does himself. It was not only during the 1990 Budget Crisis that Bush demonstrated that he cared more about the country than he did himself, but also in his last State of the Union Address, on January 28, 1992, *(See Chapter IV, Page 204),* when he said:

> And let's be frank. Let's be frank. Let me level with you. I know and you know that my plan is unveiled in a political season. I know and you know that everything I propose

will be viewed by some in merely partisan terms. But I ask you to know what is in my heart, and my aim is to increase our nation's good. I'm doing what I think is right: I am proposing what I know will help.

I pride myself that I'm a prudent man and I believe that patience is a virtue. But I understand that politics is, for some, a game — and that sometimes the game is to stop all progress and then decry the lack of improvement. **But let me tell you: far more important than my political future — and far more important than yours — is the well-being of our country.** Members of this chamber are practical people, and I know you won't resent some practical advice. When people put their party's fortunes — whatever the party, whatever side of this aisle — before the public good, they court defeat not only for their country, but for themselves. And they will certainly deserve it. [Emphases added].

The budget deficit may not compare to the crises that Lincoln, Ford or Jefferson faced but the principle of leadership and the personal courage it took for President Bush to follow his conscience in serving the public interest instead of falling to public pressure is an attribute and a model of Presidential leadership that needs to be recognized. The overall success of this great country has been based on our political leaders who were willing to do the right thing when it counted.

CHAPTER III

GOVERNANCE V. POLITICS

The complexities of the 1990 budget deal and the way it was carried out reveal the character of modern politics and the difficulties a President faces in trying to implement good governance. Bush's attempt to implement his economic policy is an example of good governance. Bush made a conscious choice between what was politically correct (not raising taxes) and what was morally correct and required of him as President (subordinating his own views when he understood it was clearly in the national interest to do so). This type of political courage and political pragmatism is an essential ingredient of effective Presidential leadership.

George Bush's victory in the 1988 Presidential election was an endorsement of the status quo and the economy produced by supply-side economics or Reaganomics. Supply-side economics is a theory that economic growth stimulated by deep tax cuts, increases revenues more than enough to offset the revenue lost by reducing taxes. Since it had been associated with a President whose tenure coincided with the longest peace time economic recovery (November 1982-July 1990) since World War II, supply-side economics became the order of the day. The down side was that supply-side economics had helped produce the fastest growing deficit in American history. During the 1988 nomination process, George Bush presented himself as the "natural heir" to the Reagan revolution while simultaneously separating himself from the past in order to gradually blend his style and **vision** for America into the Reagan success story. The only economic policy mandate President Bush received derived from his pledge that there would be "no new taxes." Bush held to his promise not to raise taxes until October, 1990, when his administration negotiated a budget agreement with Congress intended to balance the budget by 1996. At that point it was clear to the President that attacking the growing deficit was more important than protecting a political statement.

Bush's belief in being a team player and his sense of loyalty to Reagan as his Vice President made him a supporter of supply-side economics during the Reagan years. Because economic growth had been so successful during the Reagan years (Chart A page 76), and because Bush had forsworn any tax increase, he continued to support supply-side economics during the first fifteen months of his administration. However, Bush's support for supply-side economics was always qualified by his dislike for the increase in deficit spending that accompanied its practice during the Reagan administration. Contrary to conservative Republicans who saw supply-side as a solution to all economic problems **(tunnel vision),** Bush saw its limitations. He also loved its strength – lower taxes. Bush's belief in the free-enterprise system made him a supporter of smaller government and lower taxes, which create more profits, stimulate business, and the economy. Bush's **flexible vision** allowed him to see the weakness within the economy, the limitations of supply-side economics, and gave him the ability to modify his actions to fit the country's needs. The need was deficit reduction; the path was through a Democratic Congress. The method was leadership – pragmatic Presidential leadership.

Politics is a game of images, and images can become reality. During the 1988 Presidential campaign, a number of Bush's advisors felt that his political image could be improved if he were made to appear more powerful, direct, and firm. Thus, the famous Clint Eastwood-like phrase, "Read my lips: no new taxes," was drafted by speech writer Peggy Noonan to enhance Bush's public image. The no new tax line also helped tie Bush to the Reagan revolution and appease the conservatives of the Republican Party. Although some within the campaign (Richard Darman, who would be Bush's director of the Office of Management and Budget or OMB) argued that the sound bite could not hold up to political reality, others in the conservative camp (Sec. of Housing and Urban Development Jack Kemp and Sen. Phil Gramm R-Tx.) felt it must and would.

The argument that, "Read my lips: no new taxes," was an impossible pledge was based on the mutual incompatibility of several givens: (1) Bush's commitments to strong defense and no cuts in social security benefits, (2) the requirements of the Gramm-Rudman-Hollings deficit reduction law, and (3) the status of entitlement programs, which made up the biggest part of the budget and were growing faster than the rate of inflation within a political system that did not have the stomach to bring about the needed reforms in the entitlement programs.

In his 1988 campaign Bush had been encouraged to propose a "flexible freeze" as his approach to balancing the budget. The "flexible freeze" would "freeze" overall spending, while being "flexible" in deciding which programs would receive an increase in funding and which programs would receive a decrease in funding in order to achieve the overall freeze. In inflation-adjusted terms, the "flexible freeze" allowed overall spending to go up to the inflation rate. The deficit would be brought into balance with the natural growth of revenues above the inflation rate from a growing economy. Because of the economic growth during the Reagan years, particularly from 1986-1988,* Bush, "felt the economy would be dynamic enough with the flexible freeze that he would not have to raise taxes," to balance the budget. Also, during the Reagan administration, the CBO estimated revenue levels for fiscal years 1990-1994 to be 19.5 percent of the GDP under the

---

*The deficit during Reagan's first year in 1981 was $79 billion and was 2.7 percent of the GDP. By 1986 the deficit had jumped to $221.2 billion and was 5.2 percent of the GDP; however, by 1988 the deficit dropped to $155.2 billion and was down to 3.2 percent of the GDP.

TOTAL OUTPUT, INCOME, AND SPENDING
GROSS DOMESTIC PRODUCT
within the 50 states=GDP

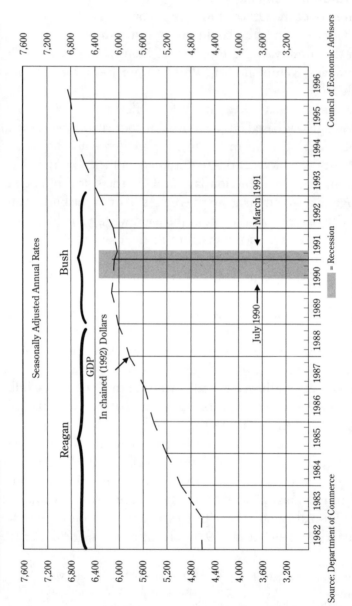

BILLIONS OF DOLLARS (RATIO SCALE)

BILLIONS OF DOLLARS (RATIO SCALE)

Seasonally Adjusted Annual Rates

Reagan   Bush

GDP

In chained (1992) Dollars

July 1990 ⟶   ⟵ March 1991

= Recession

Source: Department of Commerce   Council of Economic Advisors

Gross Domestic Product consists of four factors that reflect TOTAL output, income and spending. These factors are: (1) personal consumption and expenditures, (2) gross business domestic investment, (3) a combination of ALL foreign imports and exports, and (4) total government spending. In other words, the GDP is the sum of the nation's cash registers as it reflects the wealth that is created in all 50 states, no matter who owns the company.

existing tax policies. Even though others intensely disagreed, Bush had enough evidence to believe the flexible freeze would work, and in theory it could – especially if the 1988 election produced a substantial increase in Republican influence with the Congress. So politically, for the period of the campaign, the "Read my lips. . . ." sound bite seemed like **good campaign rhetoric** and **politics** although history showed otherwise. Even the November 21, issue of Time Magazine stated after the 1988 election that, "George Bush's last and greatest mission has now been defined: he is charged with taking command of the Reagan Revolution, adjusting its course a bit, and guiding it safely into the 1990's." Thus when "no new taxes" is put into the proper economic context and viewed from the reality of politics and how the political process operates, it was, at the time, a reasonable statement.

The problem for Bush and the country with the "flexible freeze" was that by 1990 entitlement programs, which included pensions, income security and health care made up 44% of the budget and were growing much faster than the rate of inflation. The national defense consumed another 24% of the budget while interest on public debt was another 15%. That left about 16% of the budget for domestic discretionary spending. But much of that was for programs that commanded increases; like crime control, border patrol, and drug abuse prevention. Since most of the easier spending reductions and tax loophole closing had already been done in the Reagan years, the no new tax policy was in trouble unless popular middle-class entitlement programs could be cut. The reluctance to radically reduce spending by Congress or even within the departments of the Bush cabinet added to the budget problem.

One ingredient of Presidential leadership is the **vision** to define the policy dilemmas facing the nation in terms of **emerging** historical situations and to suggest solutions that can win widespread support. By early 1990, Bush saw the emerging historical pattern of the structural budget deficit problem and the **long term solution** to America's economic success was **deficit reduction.** Four events had moved the country's deficit problem to center stage: (1) by July of 1990 the country had moved into a recession, (2) the deficit was up by almost $66 billion from when Bush took office, (3) the tightening of the money supply by the Federal Reserve helped to slow the economy and (4) the possibility of a legally mandated sequester would be triggered in October if the necessary deficit reductions were not enacted. Even the Business Roundtable put out a statement that read: " the budget deficit is the number one economic issue that the nation faces."

Because the federal government was overspent and underfinanced, the deficit issue was beginning to be recognized by members of both parties as the country's most serious economic problem. Two factors made any solution difficult. First, the Democrats who controlled Congress had no philosophical or political interest in reducing spending. Second, there existed a deep-seated conflict among Republicans about the issue of "no new taxes." With the vision to see the emerging patterns and the long-term solution, but faced with few options and little wiggle room and the responsibility of governing, Bush had to support a budget agreement that balanced the differences among the views within the Republican party, the Democratically controlled Congress, and the needs of the country. Bush's personal tendencies towards moderation and compromise made him the perfect candidate for the job.

The foundation for a presidential-congressional budget summit was laid on March 11, 1990, when the Ways and Means Chairman, Dan Rostenkowski, D-Il., unveiled a package that included "a freeze on all cost-of-living increases, including Social Security, and a fifteen-cent-per-gallon gasoline tax increase." Rep. Bill Frenzel, R-Mn., the ranking House Republican on the Budget Committee commended Rostenkowski, "For his willingness to take action, even very unpopular action. . . Rostenkowski has shown the way to a presidential-congressional summit."

On March 28, Bush met with the Republican leaders to discuss the idea of convening a "summit." House Republican leaders agreed, and on April 29 Richard Darman outlined his plan in a memo to Bush which he called "BUBBA– an acronym for Budget:

Big Bipartisan Agreement." The BUBBA memo concluded that Congress would not produce deficit reduction on its own accord and that without reductions the deficit would continue to increase and the size of the sequester by October would be politically prohibitive. The sequester would also lead to a lame duck session of Congress and a possible shutdown of the government. The memo stated that, "long-term interest rates were inching up, and that pressure on capital markets may keep inching rates up – unless there is either an economic downturn or BUBBA." Finally the memo called for Presidential **leadership** when it stated, "It's time to start the process moving seriously toward BUBBA. Delay would not be good in terms of political risks, economic risks, or opportunity costs."

Consequently, on May 1 and 2 Bush scheduled a secret meeting with the four congressional leaders: Senate Majority Leader George Mitchell and House Speaker Tom Foley representing the Democrats, and Republican leaders Senator Bob Dole and Representative Bob Michel. The purpose of the meeting was to get BUBBA started procedurally and lay a foundation for a larger and politically more representative group of congressional leaders. This larger group when formed on May 15, would consist of twenty-six congressional leaders. The larger group was not only to include the bipartisan leaders and key committee chairmen, but also four leadership selections in order to get Senator Phil Gramm, R-Tx., and House Whip Newt Gingrich, R-GA., involved. Their presence was desirable not only because of their influence within the legislative process, but also because of their ties with the Republican right. On any deal that might have to include an increase in taxes, Bush wanted them involved.

On May 6 a group of eight, which included the four congressional leaders along with Treasury Secretary Nicholas Brady, Chief of Staff John Sununu, and Director of the Office of Management and Budget Richard Darman met secretly with Bush at the White House. Darman briefed the group about the problem of the worsening sequester and the costs of stalemate. The group agreed that on

May 9 the process would formally begin with an announcement of a meeting of the group of eight, and an expanded group of twenty-six to be convened promptly at the White House to start intensive negotiations. As early as May 11, Bush in talking with the press, made it quite clear that there would be no preconditions to the negotiations, "My position is I make this offer to sit down in good faith and talk with no conditions." At this early stage Bush was well aware of the political risk he was taking on his willingness to negotiate away his no tax pledge on behalf of good government. Richard Darman makes this point quite clear when he recounts an April 29 meeting in his book, *Who's in Control?*:

> As our meeting ended, the President said, 'Well, fellas; we're on the right track.' He then paused and added conspicuously under his breath, 'From a **good-government** standpoint, that is!' Always quick with a rejoinder, Sununu offered a facetiously consoling thought: 'Remember, there have been lots of great one-term Presidents!' The four of us laughed.

The meeting of the larger group of twenty-six began on May 15 under Bush's direction and went well. On May 17 when the meeting continued, the Democrats wanted Bush to go on television to explain the problems with the deficit and the possible sequester. Bush made it clear that he would only address the nation after an agreement was reached. A month went by without much progress as neither side was willing to go first in presenting any serious proposals for fear of weakening its position or that the other side would leak it to the press. The political sensitivity of the issue made the negotiators nervous and unwilling to be accountable or act decisively. During this period both Gramm and Gingrich indicated a willingness to compromise as Gingrich stated, "I can imagine a five-year package where I try to sell taxes," but petty politics came into play and Darman felt "the whole process seemed on the verge of becoming a Big Bipartisan Embarrassment." Consequently, on June 22, Darman informed Bush "a satisfactory deal cannot be put together for announcement before the July [congressional] recess.... The big negotiating group is insufficient to do the job. A top leadership group will also have to get in on the act."

The pressure was on. Congress would recess from June 29-July 10, and by law the President is required to publish details by July 15 of the prospective sequester if a budget agreement is not reached with Congress. As a result of these time lines, Bush stated in his June 22 meeting with Darman that he wanted to go to the public with a plan and then blame Congress for the sequester, but he was convinced by Sununu that the smaller leadership group of eight could work a deal. Before meeting with the leadership group of eight, Bush met with all the Republican negotiators on Monday, June 25. At the meeting Gramm stated, "I'm very concerned our Republicans'll panic in sequester. . . . If we can get a deal, we ought to take it. If we've got to do a little bit in taxes to get a deal, do it. . . . Just don't break the pledge until there's a deal. . . ." On the same note Gingrich said, "There's no way you can deal with income tax rates," but he implied that other tax increases would be acceptable. The general feedback Bush received from the rest of the Republican negotiators was that some kind of tax increase in combination with a restraint in entitlements was a practical necessity. With this advice from the Republican leaders, Bush entered into negotiations with the smaller bipartisan leadership group of eight on June 26.

The tone and significance of the meeting that took place the morning of June 26 was reflected in Darman's opening comments to start the meeting, "With good will, there is an agreement to be reached here that is good, perhaps essential, for the country." All agreed that it was time to negotiate. Failure would mean an undesirable lame duck session of Congress. When Bush asked the three Democrats what they proposed, both Senate Majority Leader George Mitchell, D-ME., and Rep. Richard Gephardt, D-MO., turned to Speaker Tom Foley. Foley was clear and to the point. He proposed that they make a public statement, agreed upon by both sides, to the effect that both the size of the deficit problem and the need for a package that can be enacted required all of the following: entitlement and mandatory program reform, tax revenue increases, growth incentives, discretionary spending reductions, orderly reductions in defense expenditures, and budget process reform to assure that any bipartisan agreement is enforceable and that the deficit problem is brought under responsible control.

When Foley finished, Bush agreed with Foley's bipartisan solution – that blame would be shared equally and that he was abandoning his, "Read my lips: no new taxes" pledge. It was then agreed that negotiations would move forward on two tracks: the group of twenty-six headed up by Gephardt would continue to meet, while the leadership group of eight would supplement the group of twenty-six, along with leaders from both the Ways and Means and Finance committees. These committee leaders would join in to deal with particularly difficult parts of the agreement as it was negotiated. The final item was to draft a statement about the committee's negotiations based on the Bush-Foley budget compromise and release it to the press. The press release was made by lunch time on the same day. *(See Chapter IV, Page 135, June 26, 1990, Press Release on Budget).*

By September 30, when the final Bush-Foley agreement was completed, President Bush made the formal budget announcement and explained the modification in his tax policy: "Sometimes you don't get it just the way you want, and this is such a time for me. But it's time we put the interest of the United States of America first and get this deficit under control." *(See Chapter IV, Page 139, September 30, 1990, Remarks Announcing Agreement).* Unfortunately for the country, the deficit problem would not be solved by this budget agreement as Bush's **vision** for the solution was not accepted. The problem for Bush was: America has developed an impatient culture with little vision to see the benefits for the future and others played politics with the public's lack of vision in this area. Consequently, the fragile coalition forged for the budget compromise would not hold.

As a result of an unexpected and bold political move by Gingrich, the political support Bush needed within his own party was not forthcoming. Gingrich helped organize a coalition of conservative Republicans and liberal Democrats to defeat the Bush-Foley budget package. On October 5, as the voting took place on the Bush-Foley compromise, budget moderates in both parties voted first, attempting to create momentum for the measure. Ten minutes into the voting, the tide began to shift as conservative House Republicans, organized by Gingrich, began to vote no. Consequently, liberal Democrats decided not to stand with Foley. Because conservative Republicans were not standing with Bush, dozens of Democrats who would have voted for the measure if their votes had been needed withheld voting until the last minute and then voted no. The compromise was defeated 254-179. Bush suffered a humiliating defeat as he needed 218 votes to pass the bill and got only 71 of 186 Republicans to support the plan. Of the 257 Democrats, 108 voted in favor of the plan. Thus, the **first budget** agreement was voted down in the House, and Bush was forced to renegotiate with the Democratic controlled Congress from a weakened position if he wanted to pass any deficit reduction bill. After the defeat of the Bush-Foley budget, Bush continued his commitment to reducing the deficit. He stated, "I will do everything in my power to encourage Congress as it struggles to bring forth the most comprehensive and significant deficit cutting plan ever." Negotiations on a second budget compromise or congressional Democratic version dragged on for two more weeks before Congress passed an imitation of the original bill on October 27, 1990. Although Bush agreed with the economic structure (pay-as-you-go budget policy that required Congress to be financially responsible for new expenditure laws they introduced, enforceable caps on federal discretionary spending, and deficit reduction) of the second budget agreement, he did not agree with the way the tax burden was distributed. However, he signed it after intense debates within his staff about whether he should veto it to keep the heat on Congress. Bush felt he had no choice but to support it if he wanted a deficit-reduction-package. After its passage Bush stated:

> All political points of view have sacrificed to bring this agreement about...needless to say I don't like raising taxes, never will, but there is a price to divided government, and that means I have had to compromise on items that I feel strongly about in order to do what I think is best for the country, and that is to reach an agreement. *(See Chapter IV, Page 181, October 27, 1990, Remarks on the Final Budget).*

When questioned by the press about his political role in the defeat of the Bush-Foley budget, Gingrich said, "This is not going down because of Newt Gingrich. . . . The reason this is in trouble is the American people." Gingrich's statement is a glittering generality of a half-truth. It is true the American people do not like tax increases or cuts in entitlement programs; however, the public dislikes recession and large deficits even more. As Jefferson once said in 1787, "The people cannot be all, and always, well informed." This is just as true today as it was in 1787. The quote applies today particularly to the public's lack of understanding about the complexities of our economy. President Bush and the Democratic leaders had the vision to understand this point; apparently Gingrich did not, as his political rhetoric played to the public's lack of vision and impatience.

In the years that followed, Bush felt the compromise budget was a **political** mistake that contributed to his defeat in his bid for reelection, while Darman felt the mistake with the budget compromise was tactical in the form of timing and presentation. Several Congressmen seemed to agree with Darman and so did the New York Times, as the following quote from an article covering a press conference on October 10, 1990, demonstrates.

> It was a characteristic . . . . for a partisan politician who was bred to believe in the Establishment's way of operating,

that important decisions are best made behind closed doors with a group of men who shared the same goals and assumptions. Mr. Bush was asked whether it would not have been better to throw open to the public a debate over a 12-cent-a-gallon gasoline tax that would have caused many Americans hardship, rather than arbitrarily agreeing in secret sessions with Congressional leadership on what was best for everyone.

The President replied: "Well, I don't know that any person who is opposed to raising gasoline taxes would have been more inclined to accept them if the negotiations between Democrats and Republicans on these committees had been done in public.

Darman and Bush were both right. The budget agreement itself was an act of good governance and not a political mistake. However, it became a political mistake because of the Bush administration's lack of public preparation and unwillingness or inability to sell the need for the agreement to the public before the November elections so that members of Congress could politically support it. The budget deal occurred just before congressional elections; consequently, it made it difficult for some members to vote their conscience. Instead, they voted for their careers. The short notice to the public also proved to be a problem. The information foundation had not been laid that was necessary to explain to the public that a complete substantive compromise on tax policy and entitlement programs had been made in order to achieve what was in the best interest of the country. Also, the secrecy did not allow members of Congress to lay an information foundation for themselves with their constituents. This point is well demonstrated by another quote from the Times on October 1, 1990, when a Democratic Senator, (unnamed in the article) involved in a difficult reelection campaign said, "I may have to vote against it and hope it passes. . . ." It is apparent that the timing of the congressional elections made it difficult for the budget compromise to succeed.

What the Times and the Democratic senator failed to recognize is that Presidents and members of Congress are elected to govern. Governing involves leading the public on issues of national concern in a direction that is in the best interest of the country and not to do just what is popular. President Bush realized this as he addressed business leaders on the federal budget agreement on October 2, 1990:

> as I look at the ever-increasing deficits, I think it is time we do something and do something serious. And with that philosophy has emerged this budget agreement. And I don't want to sound sanctimonious about this, but I was elected to govern. *(See Chapter IV, Page 159, October 2, 1990, Remarks to Business Leaders).*

Bush realized and history has shown that the Bush-Foley budget agreement, defeated in Congress on October 5, 1990, was a down payment or the **first step** by both the President and Congress on agreeing to swallow a bitter pill to cure an economy that by all accounts was seriously ill.

> I think – respecting the differences that do exist not only in this room but in the Congress – I think we all realize the time has come to get America's fiscal house in order. And I honestly believe – and this is what I came over to tell you – that this compromise is a major step towards this goal. *(See Chapter IV, Page 160, October 2, 1990, Remarks to Business Leaders).*

The **second step** came on October 27, 1990, when Congress passed and Bush signed (November 5, 1990), the congressional Democratic version or second compromise bill which was not as beneficial for the economy, but was still a major step in the right direction. The Clinton budget in August of 1993 was the **third step** which continued the economic recovery started by the Bush administration – which is still in progress in 1998 – in March of 1991.

In comparing the difference between the **first step** (Bush-Foley) and the **second step** (the congressional Democratic version) there is no doubt the **first step** was a better proposal in trying to repair the economy. However, it is important to understand that both budget proposals included the four KEY elements to economic recovery that Bush wanted: (1) five-year budgeting; which meant budget resolutions had to project spending revenues, and deficits for five years, (2) a pay-as-you-go budget policy that required Congress to be financially responsible for new expenditure laws they introduced, (3) enforceable caps on federal discretionary spending, and (4) deficit reduction. By any measure, both budget proposals were the most ambitious efforts ever to curb federal spending. For example, it was the first time in our history that an enforceable cap had been placed on federal discretionary spending. As a result, appropriation bills had to stay within specific caps for defense, foreign aid, and domestic discretionary spending for fiscal 1991-1993; for fiscal 1994-1995, the law set overall discretionary spending caps. Bills exceeding the caps would be out of order for floor consideration unless accompanied by offsetting cuts or revenue increases. Each year these caps were to be adjusted upward to account for inflation. Besides the first three keys to economic recovery, deficit reduction in both bills required new entitlement, mandatory spending, and tax initiatives to be paid for at the time they were voted upon. Both bills also provided cuts of almost $500 billion dollars, which included **net** tax increases of $134 billion for the **first step** budget and $137.2 billion for the **second step.** At the same time the **second step** budget agreement provided for $99 billion in savings by substantially reforming the mandatory entitlements programs for veterans, students, farmers, federal employees, and the Medicare population, and reduced subsidies in programs that ranged from public housing to the Postal Service.

The tax elements of the **first step** were less than half the size of the tax increases signed by President Reagan in 1982. Also, the **first step** left income tax rates as they were under current law (something Gingrich said was a must), but did increase consumption taxes on gas, heating oil, cigarettes, alcohol, luxury goods, and aviation fees in the form of a tax on passenger plane tickets. For small businesses, Bush's **first step** agreement provided tax breaks and enterprise zones that amounted to $18.1 billion over five years to encourage investment, research, and production.

The **second step** agreement saw only $773 million in tax incentives for small business instead of the $18.1 billion provided in the **first step** agreement. The **second step** also provided for a tax increase averaging 6.4 percent on the wealthiest one percent of taxpayers, those with incomes of more than $200,000 a year. Those with incomes below $20,000 received a modest tax cut. Those with incomes in between received tax increases in the neighborhood of two percent. Finally, the **second step** did include a small reduction on the top tax rate from 33 percent to 31 percent.

Before the **second step** agreement, taxpayers either paid a 15 percent or a 28 percent rate; however, certain taxpayers were subject to a so-called "bubble tax" of 33 percent. Because of their high income, these taxpayers would pay the 28 percent, plus they would have personal exemptions and other tax benefits phased out to swell their actual rate up to 33 percent. The **second step** agreement repealed this so-called "bubble tax." Instead, those paying the 33 percent rate were subject to the new 31 percent. Before the **second step** took effect, taxpayers paid the same tax rate on capital gains income as they did on ordinary income. The **second step** set the maximum capital gains tax rate at 28 percent. Thus, those who paid the 33 percent rate would get a tax reduction. Business groups that had been pushing a capital gains tax cut dismissed the change as too insignificant to have much effect on investment. Bush had proposed the rate be reduced to 15 percent, so they were naturally disappointed.

Bush was highly criticized by conservative Republicans for signing the **second step** budget. However, if they would have supported Bush on the **first step** budget agreement, there would never have been an increase in the personal tax rate during his Presidency. Bush had few options as he faced large opposition control of both houses of Congress. Also, Republicans were divided and did not have the power in Congress to stop or modify the Democrat's version of the budget. The public could not suffer because members of Congress needed to play politics during an election year or were caught between loyalty and duty to constituents in their district or state versus loyalty to the nation – the **two Congress theory.** So when Congressional Democratic leaders Foley, Mitchell, and Gephardt were willing to go against the traditional Democratic flow and cut entitlements, and Congressional Republican leaders Dole and Michel were willing to go against the traditional Republican flow and raise taxes, Bush had no alternative but to support the **second step** budget. The country had to move on. Unlike the **first step** agreement, the **second step** was not all good governance. Acutely aware that Bush and Ronald Reagan before him had painted Democrats into a corner on tax issues in the past three presidential campaigns, Democrats stressed their preference for more progressive revenue measures that would place a greater burden on business and upper-income taxpayers. Congressional Democrats also admitted privately that a rate hike would also be the most direct way to remind voters that Bush had to renounce his "no new tax" pledge to deal with the deficit problem.

Why was the budget agreement so necessary to Bush and the country? Part of the answer is found in the magnitude of the problem. It took almost two hundred years for the national debt to reach one trillion dollars. In 1981 the debt was 994.8 billion and it took only eleven years more (1992) to reach four trillion.

Another reason for the actions of both the Democratic and Republican leaders was their pragmatic and visionary leadership, leadership that was able to recognize that what mattered most was not that they had changed their minds on a key political issue, but that they had the **vision** to do what was in the best interest of the country. House Speaker Tom Foley's comments made in support of

the **first step** budget during the debate over its approval illustrates this **vision** and the importance of the agreement. Foley
stated that the Congress had

> to deal with a critical problem we have all ignored too
> long. Members of the Congress have ignored it, members
> of both parties have ignored it, Presidents have ignored it.
> And over the period of recent years, in the life of those who
> have served in this body – and within the time of their
> service – the interest on the Federal debt has grown to a
> figure now third-largest of all the expenditures in the Fed-
> eral budget. And greater, significantly enough, than the
> entire budget was only a few years ago [1969]. The prob-
> lem is not divided into a Republican problem and a De-
> mocratic problem; it is a problem that faces all of us. It
> faces the country and it affects every American.

For conservative Republicans, however, ideology became more
important than running a government. These Republicans did not
have the **vision** to see the possible economic consequences of their
actions nor the understanding to appreciate the ineffectiveness and
loss of leverage in bargaining power that a political defeat of this
nature would have on a sitting President. The actions of Gingrich
and the conservative Republicans might have given insight to the
Democrats. The passage of President Bill Clinton's **step three**
budget in 1993 occurred only after Senator Bob Kerrey, D-NE.,
announced his support of the Clinton budget in a dramatic fashion on the floor of the Senate. Before casting his vote Kerry addressed Clinton and said "I could not and should not cast a vote
that brings down your presidency." Kerry's vote created a 50-50 tie
and allowed Vice President Al Gore to break the tie. Bush and the
moderate Republican leaders had negotiated the best budget
package they could with a Democratically controlled Congress.
The unwillingness of conservative Republicans to compromise, or
their lack of vision in understanding this country's political

process and the complexity of the political problems created for Bush and the economy can only be viewed as shortsightedness, or a self-serving grab for political power. An illustration of this shortsightedness about the **first step** budget is found in a quote from the Times on October 5, 1990, from Representative Bud Shuster, R-PA: "It is sheer folly for us to impose on the American people a $134 billion tax increase when we're on the brink of recession."

The sheer folly came for Newt Gingrich and the conservative Republicans like Shuster when Congress passed the **second step** budget which included $137.2 billion net (the budget called for $164.6 billion in new taxes, offset by $27.4 billion in tax breaks) in new "taxes" and increased the personal income tax rate from a high of 28 percent to 31 percent. The political irony is that it appeared that Gingrich was the winner in the battle over the budget and that his philosophy prevailed, but the reality was **he gambled and lost what he stood for:** no increase in the personal income tax rates. Unlike Bush, Gingrich was a winner as his personal prestige and political power increased tremendously. Gingrich helped knock a sitting Republican President out of office and then was elected Speaker of the House as he pulled off the Republican congressional takeover of 1994 and was named "Man of the Year" by Time magazine.

With the exception of Gingrich, the group of twenty-six negotiators agreed the compromise was not perfect, would be politically unpopular, but was nonetheless essential for the good of the country. The theory behind BUBBA was that if the bipartisan leaders would agree and stand together to take the political heat, the necessary legislation could be passed and the public interest served. If Gingrich and the conservative Republicans would have supported Bush and the Congressional leadership on the **first step** budget, the strength of the bipartisan support would have provided the energy necessary for Bush to acquire the public's understanding. This type of public forgiveness was seen in 1984 and 1996 after both Reagan and Clinton violated tax pledges they had made in their respective campaigns in 1980 and 1992 and were nonetheless reelected. If the **first step** budget had passed, this **vision** demonstrated by Bush and the Congressional Democratic leaders could have been reinforced with constant and consistent statements by Bush and his administration that this budget was the **key** to the future. If the Bush administration had continued to stress that **both Democrats and Republicans had the vision** to see the compromise was the short term solution to establishing **long-term** success for the economy, Bush's chances for re-election in 1992 would have been much higher.

John Sununu's comment helps explain the significance not only of the **first step,** but of all **three steps** between 1990-1993: "The most important impact of this (the Bush-Foley budget agreement) is as a contributor to the overall economic climate." The key point Sununu made was that the economic climate would be determined by whether the financial markets perceived the budget deal to be a credible deal that the President and Congress would keep, or as more election politics of "smoke and mirrors." An indication that the financial markets viewed the budget package favorably is reflected in a comment by Alan Greenspan, Chairman of the Federal Reserve Board: "Congress has crafted what appears to be a credible, enforceable reduction in the budget deficit over a number of years. . . ." and failure to approve the deal would be "a grave mistake."

Greenspan felt the budget deal would have a positive impact on interest rates because long-term interest rates, which move in accordance with market expectations of inflation, would be forced down as a result of the **first step** budget package and the Federal Reserve could then follow by cutting the short-term rates. Greenspan implied to the Bush administration that if the budget agreement were passed, the Federal Reserve would move to lower interest rates – and it did after Bush signed the **second step** budget. The following quote from Bush illustrates, that the indications he received from Greenspan that interest rates would be lowered, which would help lead to economic recovery, if a budget agreement were reached was one of the motivating factors for his decision to approve the **second step** budget:

> The economy is sluggish, and there's no question about that. And I am convinced, whether I like every paragraph of this or not, that this is good medicine for the economy, particularly if the Federal Reserve board now follows up with lowering interest rates. You know, that is what's needed, and I'm not here to do anything other than to state that principle. *(See Chapter IV, Page 189, October 27, 1990, Press Conference: Remarks on the Final Budget).*

Besides lower interest rates, business expansion is also tied to expectations of future sales. The history of economic development demonstrates that business and the public respond either positively or negatively depending upon their view of the overall economic climate. Hence, the significance of Greenspan's remarks and actions, as well as the dropping of long-term interest rates, as predicted, had a favorable impact on the economic climate. Any time a President and Congress convince the general public and the financial markets that they have produced a credible budget deal, the economic climate within the country will become more positive, thereby, creating positive expectations about future sales and the economy. As this happens, the deficit and short and long term interest rates will continue to drop helping to ease the inflation rate. As the deficit drops, the federal government competes less with the private sector for available loanable funds, reducing demand for these funds, thus pushing interest rates down. A second aspect is that if the federal government "crowds-out" the private sector for the loanable funds, there is less capital available for business investment which makes business expansion difficult and expensive. With the deficit, interest rates, and inflation moving in a downward direction, there will be an increase in capital outlays and improvements by American business that will **in time** create more jobs. In summary, the 1990 budget agreement was a **catalyst** that produced a chain of events that started economic recovery.

The problem for the Bush administration, as the 1992 election proved, was that it was not widely recognized by the public or the press that Congress and the President had produced a credible budget deal. Consequently, only as the economic recovery that started in March of 1991 produced tangible, broadly felt benefits during the second half of Clinton's first term, did the public begin to understand the significance of the budget agreements. By late 1997 and early 1998, open minded individuals began to recognize the legacy of George Bush and the **second step** budget agreement. Dan Rostenkowski, who chaired the tax-writing House Ways and Means Committee for thirteen years, and was therefore the most influential member in Congress on tax matters stated in a January interview with NBC's "Meet the Press": "I have to take my hat off to George Bush because the threshold of today's economic prosperity was laid in the 1990 tax increases that George Bush had the courage to put on the books."

Because the economic recovery, following the passage of the 1990 budget agreement, was slower than anticipated, the current recovery and the 1990 budget agreements have been subjected to much criticism. Conservative Republicans claimed the slow growth in the 1991-1996 economy was attributed to higher taxes. However, by 1997 the steady economic growth was undeniable to any observer. Historically, higher taxes during a stagnated economy have created a recession or deepened an existing recession. Thus, the question is WHY did higher taxes during the second and third budget agreements help lead to economic recovery?

The answer and what became **the four keys to economic recovery** is that the higher taxes were tied into a tax package that called for both **enforceable caps on federal discretionary spending** and **a pay-as-you-go budget policy.** These elements, along with the higher taxes, brought about the third element – **deficit reduction** which led to the recovery. The difference between the 1991-2000 recovery and the traditional historical pattern is that the growth occurred because the deficit dropped,

which helped lower unemployment, kept interest rates and inflation low, and thus provided for a healthy enough economy to get
Clinton reelected in 1996. Economic growth would not have occurred if the deficit had not been cut and the deficit would not
have been cut unless there had been cuts in government spending,
particularly entitlements, and no cuts in entitlements would have
taken place without tax increases. Consequently, it has been a combination of positive factors which stimulated economic growth
(reduced deficit, low interest and inflation rates, and the development of a favorable attitude within the financial markets) and a
negative factor that traditionally stunts economic growth (tax increases) that have provided a **blended** economic reaction of slow
but steady growth.

The argument that deficit reduction leads to recovery is opposed by both supply-side and Keynesian economists who hold
that recovery leads to deficit reductions. From the beginning of the
recovery in March, 1991, to the end of fiscal year 1995, supply-
side and Keynesian economics could not contribute to the recovery. Keynesian economic theory requires increased government
spending and tax reductions during a recession to stimulate the
economy. Hence, Keynesian practices would have exacerbated the
deficit problem. Consequently, the size of the deficit and the structural budget deficit problem inherited by the Bush administration
did not simply limit Bush's flexibility to fight the recession by way
of tax cuts and deficit spending; it made it impossible.

As demonstrated during the Reagan years, instead of following the Keynesian economic theory of raising taxes and lowering
debt during good times, Congress had habitually continued to
deficit spend during good times as well as bad. This process passes
the burden of debt to the next generation and erodes its quality of
life as governmental funds are used for interest payments instead
of better roads and schools. Also, the budget deficit during the
1980's became so large that domestic saving could no longer provide the capital to service the debt. Consequently, the government

borrowed from foreign sources to make up the difference. This situation raises the small possibility of a "stabilization crisis," which can occur if foreign investors lose confidence in the dollar and liquidate their U.S. investments. Such a crisis could cause interest rates and inflation to accelerate rapidly.

The supply-side theory would not work because the structural budget deficit problem allowed entitlement programs to grow faster than the rate of the country's economic growth, eating-up any additional tax revenue stimulated by the economic growth. The concepts behind the Bush-Foley budget agreement did work. By 1996, with the recovery well underway, the increase in revenues above what was projected by the government reduced the deficit to an unexpected low of $107 billion despite the **second step** tax increase of $137 billion and the **third step** tax increase of $177 billion (both spread over five years). With the economic recovery continuing throughout 1997, the deficit for fiscal year 1997 dropped to $22.6 billion. On September 30, 1998, when the Federal government closed its books for fiscal year 1998, the budget showed a surplus of 69.2 billion; it was the first time since 1969 the budget showed a surplus. By September 30, 1999 the budget surplus had increased to $122.7 billion.

What is important to keep in mind is that the **first step** of the recovery process was started as a result of President Bush's leadership, political courage, and **flexible vision.** But, because the economy was already in a recession for three months before the **second step** (October 27, 1990) and five months before its key provisions went into effect (January 1, 1991), the positive impact of the **second step** was not immediately felt and looked like an utter failure to the public, members of Congress, and at times to Bush himself. This sense of failure developed as the real per capita income declined by one percent in 1991 as compared to a 3 percent increase during the 1988 Reagan economy; unemployment continued to increase from 5.5 percent in 1988 to 7.5 percent in 1992, and the deficit went to an all time high of $290.4 billion in 1992.

A number of other factors contributed to the public's negative perception of the economy. The first was the burden of the **second step,** the increased taxes and program cuts were felt immediately. Next, the economic growth in 1992 did not meet the rosy political revenue projections of the 1990 budget; consequently, there was a short fall in projected tax revenues. High revenue projections made during the **second step** are typical of congressional leaders fond of creating optimistic budget figures. They hoped the optimistic budget figures would make the political pain less for themselves while giving the appearance of less economic pain for the general public. Consequently, Congress, not Bush, gave the public the false impression that it had produced a better short term solution for the economy than it actually had.

Another factor contributing to the public's negative perception was its high expectations for economic growth. During Reagan's last year in office, 1988, the Real Gross Domestic Product (Real GDP) was 3.80 percent, a stark contrast to the negative one percent decline in the GDP in 1991. Finally, the deficit did continue to grow. It grew in part because the impact of lower interest rates can take from nine to twelve months or even more before the **real** economy is affected. Also, $132.1 billion was needed by tax payers for the Savings and Loan Bailout, a legacy from the Reagan Presidency, and the $56.5 billion spent on the Gulf War in 1991.

The recession started in July, 1990, and was over by March of 1991. Although unrecognized and unappreciated by the public, by 1992 the economy was in recovery as real GDP experienced a growth rate of 2.72 percent and real per capita disposable personal income rose from a negative growth rate of one percent in 1991 to a positive growth rate of 1.7 percent. Yet this, along with the fact that interest rates continued to drop and inflation stayed close to 4 percent, made little difference in the public's negative attitude about the economy.

Studies of government and economic cycles show a new President's economic policies do not affect the economy until he has been in office for about 18 months. One reason this is true is because for the first year the new President is operating under a budget that is not his. A President's first budget is approved in September of his first year and goes into effect on October first of that year. Thus, it is not until the middle of his second year that the economic and social polices established during his administration are felt. In this context, the economic growth that was reported by the Commerce Department for 1993 was a reflection on the economic decisions made eighteen or more months earlier. For 1993, the Department reported the GDP had grown 2.9%, with a robust 5.9% growth rate for the fourth quarter, the greatest GDP growth in five years. When the 1993 GDP figures were released a Clinton White House spokesman, Mark Gearan, said, "we're delighted," and attributed the growth to the administration's deficit-reduction program, which he said resulted in lower interest rates. Gearan was right; the economic growth was a result of the administration's deficit-reduction program – President Bush's administration.

The economicc performance in 1993 was in large measure a product of the Bush era and the 1990 budget agreement. Note that in 1993, the deficit dropped by 35 billion, interest rates and inflation continued to drop and the unemployment rate dropped:

Year	Deficit in Billions of Dollars	Prime Rate	Unemployment Rate	Inflation Rate	% Change in Real Per Capita Disposable Personal Income	Real Rate of Economic Growth or GDP
1988	155.2	9.32	5.5	4.9	3.00	3.80
1989	152.5	10.87	5.3	6.7	1.00	3.37
1990	221.2	10.01	5.6	5.5	.80	1.29
1991	269.4	8.46	6.8	4.1	-1.00	-1.00
1992	290.4	6.25	7.5	4.2	1.70	2.72
1993	255.1	6.00	6.9	3.7	.10	2.27

One of the causes of the public's lack of appreciation for the improvement in some economic indicators is the **economic lag factor.** There is always a lag in time between the reality of the economic conditions and the change in the public's attitudes and actions by way of their spending and investing patterns. It takes time for financial markets and the general public to feel and to recognize the economic changes which occur. For example, the economy, whether moving into a recession or recovery, does not feel the immediate impact on employment because job opportunities respond to economic events after they occur. Employers give more over-time to regular employees or hire on a part-time basis new workers until they feel confident enough about the economy to expand their labor force. One of the two reasons why unemployment figures dropped during the Clinton administration and not during the Bush administration was this lag time in investment and employers' decisions. The second reason for the down turn in unemployment figures was that Clinton continued the process of economic recovery by getting Congress to pass his budget **(step three)** which lowered the deficit and kept interest rates down. Thus, the economic foundation that was laid during the Bush Presidency provided the launching pad for the Clinton economy.

The concept of lagging economic recovery and how the public perceives the economy is further demonstrated by the ebb and flow of Bush's popularity in the Gallup poll. As mentioned, the recession started in July, 1990 and was over by March of 1991. Bush's approval rating stood at 60 percent in the last Gallup poll before Iraq's invasion of Kuwait in August, 1990. Two weeks after the invasion Bush's rating had jumped to 75 percent and peaked in March in 1991 at 89 percent when the recession was over. Late in 1991, after the economy had moved to the forefront in people's thinking, Bush's approval rating dropped below 50 percent. In 1992, Bush's approval rating averaged 40 percent even though economic indicators such as the real GDP, real per capita disposable personal income, inflation rate and interest rates all showed improvements over the 1990 recessionary economy. One of the explanations for these poor approval ratings and the public's lagging attitude about the economy is that recessions end at their lowest point and recoveries begin at this same point. Consequently, the public still feels a recession even though the economy is moving in a positive direction. Not until the economy has made substantial improvements does the public feel the effect of the recovery.

The lack of understanding by the public about the **political lag factor** also contributed to the public's lack of appreciation for Bush's leadership. There is always a lag in time between the time a problem occurs in society and the political action taken by Congress and the President. The lag time is tied to the complexity of the event and whether it is political, social, or economic. In most cases economic events have a longer lag time because it takes three consecutive months of economic downturn to have a recession. The political lag factor with economic events has a three step process. The *first step* is to recognize the problem and decide if the problem will be self correcting or only a mild downturn. Once it has been widely recognized that the country is in a recession, at least four to five months have passed. The *second step* includes analyzing the recession, trying to decide what caused the recession, and deciding what action should be taken. The second step can take at least another month or two because of the complexity of our economy and its relationship to the world economy. Finally, the *third step* consists of developing the solution, selling it to a Congress that may be controlled by the opposition party or who find the solution technically correct but politically unacceptable, and coming up with a politically acceptable solution for both Democrats and Republicans. As demonstrated with the 1990 budget agreement, the third step can take five to six months. Hence, the shortest period in which any administration can be expected to publicly recognize a recession, develop an acceptable solution, and sell it to the opposition party and the public is ten to twelve months. The Bush administration's response to the 1990-1991 recession was within that time period. The political problem for Bush developed because of the economic lag and other factors, and not because he did not have the ability to see the problem or the vision to see the solution.

It is said timing is everything; the Bush administration's timely response to the recession was not planned by the administration, but occurred because Bush had the ability to identify the structural budget deficit problem as the emerging economic problem facing the nation. The recession started in July, 1990. Bush had already decided by the end of April, 1990, that his "no new tax" pledge must go because he foresaw the economic problems the deficit would cause. As the recession developed, it convinced Bush even more that deficit reduction was the number one domestic issue facing the nation. Consequently, Bush realized he would have to pay whatever price was necessary to get a budget agreement that would produce deficit reduction. Bush's ability to see the emerging economic pattern caused by the structural budget deficit problem and his willingness to try to change that pattern gave the country a jump-start on fighting the 1990-1991 recession. The jump-start shortened the lag time and made the economic recovery begin sooner.

The public's negative attitude about the Bush economy was also shaped by the press and its unwillingness to cover positive aspects of the economy when they occurred. Studies of the media's affect conclude that the press helps to set the country's political agenda by influencing what is uppermost in the minds of policy-makers and the American people. People who have lost their jobs do not have to be told that unemployment is a problem. As unemployment rates continued to increase during the Bush administration, more and more people could feel its economic impact which contributed to their political frustration. The press used its agenda-setting power to play on the economic negatives as the news item of the day. Instead of creating a feeling of hope and building a mild positive change in attitude about the economy over positive factors, the media helped to undermine the positive in the economy by stressing the negative. Because of the public's lack of understanding of the economic and political lag factors, and as the negative elements within the economy undermined public support for Bush's public policy his performance as a legitimate leader came under question. Bush's inability to overcome the agenda-setting power of the press and to convince the public that the economy was in recovery were major reasons for his defeat in 1992.

The wisdom of using the **four keys to economic recovery** (five-year budgeting, a pay as you go budget policy, enforceable caps on federal discretionary spending, and deficit reduction) developed by the Bush administration was later supported with modifications by President Bill Clinton. In August of 1993 President Clinton signed into law what he called, "the largest deficit reduction in history." Although Bush could not agree with many parts of Clinton's budget, the concepts of pay-as-you-go, caps on discretionary spending, and deficit reduction struck a resemblance to the key elements of both of the 1990 budget agreements. Even though the budget agreement was the right approach in dealing with the economy, the problem for Bill Clinton and the 1994 Democratic Congress, which passed the Clinton bill, was that this approach was not understood or politically unacceptable to the American people as was evidenced in the 1994 Congressional election.

The significance of the **three step** budget process is that it was part of a painful political growth process for the Presidency, Congress, and the American people that was needed in order to have the recovery and the economic stability that is apparent today. Although Bush was not aware of it at the time, the road to economic recovery would take more than the **first step** budget agreement. In his address to the nation on October 2, 1990, President Bush tried to prepare the public for the hard road ahead if his **first step** budget agreement was not passed. He stated:

> For the first time, a Republican President and leaders of a Democratic Congress have agreed to real cuts that will be enforced by law, not promises − no smoke, no mirrors, no magic act, but real and lasting spending cuts.

> Year after year, it [the deficit] mortgages the future of our children. No family, no nation can continue to do business the way the Federal Government has been operating and

survive. When you get a bill, that bill must be paid. And when you write a check, you're supposed to have money in the bank. But if you don't obey these simple rules of common sense, there's a price to pay.

But for too long, the Nation's business in Washington has been conducted as if these basic rules did not apply. Well, these rules do apply. And if we fail to act, next year alone we will face a Federal budget deficit of more than $300 billion, a deficit that could weaken our economy further and cost us thousands of precious jobs. If what goes up must come down, then the way down could be very hard. *(See Chapter IV, Page 165, October 2, 1990, Address to the Nation)*

It is important to understand that the significance of the second step was that it slowed the growth of the deficit and set the stage for the third step, or the Clinton budget, which cut the deficit from $255.1 billion in 1993 to $22.6 billion by October of 1997 – the effect everyone thought the first or second step budgets would have had. Without the first step, the second step would not have happened, and without the second step the third step would have only initiated the economic recovery; consequently, neither Clinton nor the American people would have enjoyed the same amount of economic progress that has been accomplished to date. Dan Rostenkowsi made this point in a January 14, 1998 interview with the Congressional Quarterly.

I like George Bush. He drove harder than anybody else to get a balanced budget and deficit reduction. Because he did that, he sacrificed himself at the polls. So I give [Bush] a great deal of credit for the economic recovery. The Republicans who are taking bows for the Bush legacy have no right to do that because they didn't support Bush.

As with many Presidents, time and history makes the wisdom of their actions appear more self-evident. This has already become the case with George Bush and his fight to reduce the deficit even though his political critics continue to disparage his vision. In an interview in Redding California, during the 1995-1996 Congressional budget crisis, the Speaker of the House, Newt Gingrich was asked, "Would there have been a government shutdown similar to what happened in 1995-1996 in 1990 if President Bush had not agreed to raise taxes?" Gingrich's response was, "Yes, and we would of had the same fight then and he still would be President." Gingrich felt Bush should have gone to the American people and said, "The Democrats want me to raise taxes. I'm going to keep my word to you. Let's have an election in November, 1990. If you want a tax increase vote Democrat. If you want a smaller government with lower taxes vote Republican. If you vote Democrat, then I'll sign the tax increase. Then you, the American people, made the decision – I suspect we would have won control in 1990."

Although Gingrich's argument appeals to democratic sentiment and in theory is very logical, it is doubtful that the American people or the Democrats would have accepted or even tolerated Bush shutting down the government to wait for the results of the November elections. In fact, during the 1996 Presidential election, the American public made it clear they were very dissatisfied with a political process that resulted in a government shutdown. If Bush had followed Gingrich's advice, under the political conditions described, he would have been held responsible just as Gingrich himself and the Republican Congress were held responsible in 1996 for the government shutdown. During the 1996 election, most Democrats and Clinton aides effectively focused political attention on the Gingrich shutdown of government. Furthermore, Bush would have been playing politics at the expense of the American people, violating his own integrity, and the integrity of the office of the Presidency for personal and political gain. People expect a President to act Presidential and take decisive action, not passively let the events of the day make the decisions for him. The public would have perceived Bush as holding the country hostage to win a congressional election; consequently, following Gingrich's advice would not only have been politically unwise, it might have been disastrous for Republicans running for election in 1990.

The difficulty of solving the problems within the economy becomes more complicated with an unsophisticated press. The press, primarily interested in information about the economy as sound bites for entertainment value, failed to identify the key economic issues for the public. For example, the deficit, the political gamesmanship of key Congressional leaders, and the impact of the Gramm-Rudman-Hollings law were all grossly neglected. The lack of the press' sophistication is also evident in their excessively negative economic reporting. During the six months from October 1990 through March 1991, according to *Media Monitor,* more than 90 percent of the descriptive terms used by reporters in connection with the economy were negative. On network television, the word "recession" accounted for three-fifths of the descriptive terms. During 1991, the American economy generated more news stories than any other domestic topic. The Bush administration, trying to evade not only the political repercussions, but the real economic repercussions from the public's negative attitude and loss of confidence about the economy that comes with a recession, avoided the use of the word "recession" and even refused to admit the country was in a recession until January, 1991. The recession was over in March, 1991.

If any President tells the country the economy is in a recession and things look bleak for the next six months to a year, he will undermine public confidence in the economy, encouraging business to wait and see, consumers to be more cautious, and thus the economic recovery to be delayed longer. As in politics, economic appearance can become reality. Thus, a President's first line of political action is to be supportive of the economy in hopes of maintaining stability and generating economic growth while at the same time he is involved in the second step of trying to decide what action to take if the recession continues. Bush's awareness of his economic influence is clear from the following: "I am concerned, but I don't want to talk ourselves into recession. The President has to be very careful in commenting on prices, on markets." *(See Chapter IV, Page 155, October 1, 1990, Remarks on Signing a Resolution for Continued Government.)* Once the strategy that the "economy is basically sound" fails, a President must move into the third step of political action by introducing new policy changes in order to produce economic recovery. As mentioned, the new policy for the Bush administration was based upon three points: a pay-as-you-go budget policy, enforceable caps on federal discretionary spending, and deficit reduction.

As stated earlier, one of the necessary tools of effective Presidential leadership is the President's ability to articulate the emerging national problems and their solutions to the public, members of Congress, and the media in a way that captures their imagination and convinces them that he is moving in the right direction. Bush's failure to communicate in a timely fashion the need for a complete and substantive compromise on tax policy and entitlement programs was a contributing factor to the failure of the Bush-Foley budget agreement. With the appropriate time to lay an informational foundation for their constituents, members of Congress **might have** been able to politically support the Bush-Foley agreement. The reasons Bush failed to communicate are three-fold. First, it must be remembered that while Bush was dealing with the budget crisis, he was preparing to deal with Saddam Hussein. Thus, the time and energy Bush put into the Persian Gulf crisis helps account for his lack of attention to political details during the budget crisis. However, Bush's lack of attention to political details cannot all be blamed on the Persian Gulf crisis.

The second reason Bush failed to communicate centers around his **modesty.** Bush felt that others can and would judge for themselves the events of the day. Like the traditional Presidents George Washington and John Adams before him, Bush saw the office of the Presidency as an opportunity for public service. Like Washington and Adams, George Bush tried to remain above politics and the political manipulation of society and its events. In this sense, this personal characteristic explains the **political flaw** in George Bush, which makes him more like the great traditional Presidents than the great modern Presidents. Those who know Bush understand this modesty and how his reluctance to boast of personal achievements is one of his more pronounced characteristics. In modern politics, modesty, or an unwillingness to sell one's programs and self, can be quite disastrous.

Finally, Bush has admitted himself that he does not have the great **communication skills** of a Ronald Reagan or an FDR. This lack of skill in combination with his unwillingness (political flaw) to package and sell his programs and himself helps explain his political short comings in his bid for re-election in 1992. These characteristic also explain Bush's failure to communicate his domestic programs and his unwillingness to use his political capital after the Persian Gulf War to take on a Democratically controlled Congress and sell his domestic programs and economic accomplishments to the public. For George Bush, his fault lies not in the fact that he did not have vision; his fault lies in the fact that he could not and would not articulate his vision in an effective way to the public. Bush's vision of lowering the deficit established his legacy to the American people in domestic policy by laying the foundation, as of April 2000, for the longest economic recovery. Although George Bush exercised political courage and pragmatism like FDR, what separates George Bush from FDR was not only FDR's willingness to sell his programs and himself, but FDR's **ability to arouse public support** for those programs.

It is clear that Bush's actions during the 1990 Congressional budget agreement reflected his belief that he was acting in the country's best interest. However, as the following quote indicates, it was NOT his personal desire to raise taxes and it is clear that it was NOT in his best political interest to go against his campaign pledge.

I don't control the Congress. I don't control either House of the Congress as the President. My party doesn't control it. But I was elected to govern. And I can stand; I can veto; I can do a lot of things. But the time, in my view, has come, because of the seriousness of the deficit, to lay aside getting it done exactly the way I want. . . and to go forward and get it put into effect. *(See Chapter IV, Page 153, October 1, 1990, Remarks on Signing a Resolution for Continued Government)*

Why would George Bush or any President go against his own political interest for the sake of the national interest when historically Congress as a body has had such difficulty performing a similar act? The answer is twofold.

The first answer can be found in the nature of the office of the Presidency itself. Historically, the office of the Presidency has created an environment where men must make decisions that might run against the very grain of their background and values. The responsibility of the office of the Presidency have helped great leaders rise above the occasion, political or otherwise, to lead the country in the right direction – even when the country does not want to go in that direction. These leaders recognize that ideology can create blinders that limit the flexibility of choice and the opportunity of finding the best answer for the nation. Bush, like Lincoln and other successful Presidents, recognized that sometimes the restraints of party and ideology have to be broken to achieve success for the nation.

The second answer is found in a word used quite frequently in President Bush's 1992 campaign – the word "character" – political character. Historically, the country has been fortunate in that the majority of men elected to the Presidency have been well supplied with political character. It also appears that historical events, along with the nature of the office, have created within the individual holding office a greater amount of political courage and character than might have been expected.

There are numerous historical examples of Presidential leadership, from John Adams and the XYZ Affair up to Gerald Ford and the pardoning of Nixon, where Presidents have forgone their personal goals and beliefs for what they believed to be in the best interest of the nation. This quality of leadership might not be politically expedient at the time, but history has demonstrated the selfless wisdom of their actions. In a 1988 interview with Doug Wead, Bush stated: ". . . the Presidency provides an incomparable opportunity for moral leadership. . . ." and that "Public service has been hurt by individuals who lack the judgement or character to put the public's business above their own self-interest."

During the 1990 Congressional budget crisis, George Bush demonstrated this kind of leadership and that he was a man of his convictions. The following quotes also helps illustrate this point: "Most importantly, this budget agreement is our last, best chance to get the Federal budget deficit under control". *(See Chapter IV, Page 160, October 2, 1990, Remarks to Business Leaders)* and "I did it because the country, frankly, is at stake here. And every once in a while in one's Presidency, I think it dawns on the incumbent of the Oval Office that you're not going to get it exactly your own way" *(See Chapter IV, Page 159, October 2, 1990, Remarks to Business Leaders)*. John F. Kennedy might have referred to Bush's actions during the 1990 budget crisis as a "profile in courage." But Bush would say, with characteristic humility, that he just did what he was elected to do.

Chapter IV

Speeches / Press Conferences of President George Bush

Acceptance Speech for the Presidency
Republican National Convention

August 18, 1988

I have many friends to thank tonight. I thank the voters who supported me. I thank the gallant men who entered the contest for the presidency this year, and who have honored me with their support. And, for their kind and stirring words, I thank Governor Tom Kean of New Jersey – Senator Phil Gramm of Texas – President Gerald Ford – and my friend, President Ronald Reagan.

I accept your nomination for President. I mean to run hard, to fight hard, to stand on the issues – and I mean to win.

There are a lot of great stories in politics about the underdog winning – and this is going to be one of them.

And we're going to win with the help of Senator Dan Quayle of Indiana – a young leader who has become a forceful voice in preparing America's workers for the labor force of the future. Born in the middle of the century, in the middle of America, and holding the promise of the future – I'm proud to have Dan Quayle at my side.

Many of you have asked, "When will this campaign really begin?" I have come to this hall to tell you, and to tell America: Tonight is the night.

For seven and a half years I have helped a President conduct the most difficult job on earth. Ronald Reagan asked for, and received, my candor. He never asked for, but he did receive, my loyalty. Those of you who saw the President's speech this week, and listened to the simple truth of his words, will understand my loyalty all these years.

But now you must see me for what I am: The Republican candidate for President of the United States. And now I turn to the American people to share my hopes and intentions, and why – and where – I wish to lead.

And so tonight is for big things. But I'll try to be fair to the other side. I'll try to hold my charisma in check. I reject the temptation to engage in personal references. My approach this evening is, as Sergeant Joe Friday used to say, "Just the facts, ma'm."

After all, the facts are on our side.

I seek the presidency for a single purpose, a purpose that has motivated millions of Americans across the years and the ocean voyages. I seek the presidency to build a better America. It is that simple – and that big.

I am a man who sees life in terms of missions – missions defined and missions completed. When I was a torpedo bomber pilot they defined the mission for us. Before we took off we all understood that no matter what, you try to reach the target. There have been other missions for me – Congress, China, the CIA. But I am here tonight – and I am your candidate – because the most important work of my life is to complete the mission we started in 1980. How do we complete it? We build it.

The stakes are high this year and the choice is crucial, for the differences between the two candidates are as deep and wide as they have ever been in our long history.

Not only two very different men, but two very different ideas of the future will be voted on this election day.

What it all comes down to is this:

My opponent's view of the world sees a long slow decline for our country, an inevitable fall mandated by impersonal historical forces.

But America is not in decline. America is a rising nation.

He sees America as another pleasant country on the UN roll call, somewhere between Albania and Zimbabwe. I see America as the leader – a unique nation with a special role in the world.

This has been called the American Century because in it we were the dominant force for good in the world. We saved Europe, cured polio, we went to the moon, and lit the world with our culture. Now we are on the verge of a new century, and what country's name will it bear? I say it will be another American century.

Our work is not done – our force is not spent.

There are those who say there isn't much of a difference this year. But America, don't let 'em fool ya.

Two parties this year ask for your support. Both will speak of growth and peace. But only one has proved it can deliver. Two parties this year ask for your trust, but only one has earned it.

Eight years ago I stood here with Ronald Reagan and we promised, together, to break with the past and return America to her greatness. Eight years later look at what the American people have produced: the highest level of economic growth in our entire history – and the lowest level of world tensions in more than fifty years.

Some say this isn't an election about ideology, it's an election about competence. Well, it's nice of them to want to play on our field. But this election isn't only about competence, for competence is a narrow ideal. Competence makes the trains run on time but doesn't know where they're going. Competence is the creed of the technocrat who makes sure the gears mesh but doesn't for a second understand the magic of the machine.

The truth is, this election is about the beliefs we share, the values we honor, the principles we hold dear.

But since someone brought up competence...

Consider the size of our triumph: A record high percentage of Americans with jobs, a record high rate of new businesses – a record high rate of real personal income.

These are the facts. And one way you know our opponents know the facts is that to attack the record they have to misrepresent it. They call it a Swiss cheese economy. Well, that's the way it may look to the three blind mice. But when they were in charge it was all holes and no cheese.

Inflation was 12 percent when we came in. We got it down to four. Interest rates were more than 21. We cut them in half. Unemployment was up and climbing, now it's the lowest in 14 years.

My friends, eight years ago this economy was flat on its back – intensive care. We came in and gave it emergency treatment: Got the temperature down by lowering regulation, got the blood pressure down when we lowered taxes. Pretty soon the patient was up, back on his feet, and stronger than ever.

And now who do we hear knocking on the door but the doctors who made him sick. And they're telling us to put them in charge of the case again. My friends, they're lucky we don't hit them with a malpractice suit!

We've created seventeen million new jobs in the pasts five years – more than twice as many as Europe and Japan combined. And they're good jobs. The majority of them created in the past six years paid an average of more than $22,000 a year. Someone better take 'a message to Michael': Tell him we've been creating good jobs at good wages. The fact is, they talk – we deliver. They promise – we perform.

There are millions of young Americans in their 20's who barely remember the days of gas lines and unemployment lines. Now they're marrying and starting careers. To those young people I say "You have the opportunity you deserve – and I'm not going to let them take it away from you."

There are millions of older Americans who were brutalized by inflation. We arrested it – and we're not going to let it out on furlough. We're going to keep the social security trust fund sound, and out of reach of the big spenders. To America's elderly I say, "Once again you have the security that is your right – and I'm not going to let them take it away from you."

I know the liberal democrats are worried about the economy. They're worried it's going to remain strong. And they're right, it is. With the right leadership.

But let's be frank. Things aren't perfect in this country. There are people who haven't tasted the fruits of the expansion. I've talked to farmers about the bills they can't pay. I've been to the factories that feel the strain of change. I've seen the urban children who play amidst the shattered glass and shattered lives. And there are the homeless. And you know, it doesn't do any good to debate endlessly which policy mistake of the '70's is responsible. They're there. We have to help them.

But what we must remember if we are to be responsible – and compassionate – is that economic growth is the key to our endeavors.

I want growth that stays, that broadens, and that touches, finally, all America, from the hollows of Kentucky to the sunlit streets of Denver, from the suburbs of Chicago to the broad avenues of New York, from the oil fields of Oklahoma to the farms of the great plains.

Can we do it? Of course we can. We know how. We've done it. If we continue to grow at our current rate, we will be able to produce 30 million jobs in the next eight years. We will do it – by maintaining our commitment to free and fair trade, by keeping government spending down, and by keeping taxes down.

Our economic life is not the only test of our success. One issue overwhelms all the others, and that is the issue of peace.

Look at the world on this bright August night. The spirit of Democracy is sweeping the Pacific rim. China feels the winds of change. New democracies assert themselves in South America. One by one the unfree places fall, not to the force of arms but to the force of an idea: freedom works.

We have a new relationship with the Soviet Union. The INF treaty– the beginning of the Soviet withdrawal from Afghanistan – the beginning of the end of the Soviet proxy war in Angola, and with it the independence of Namibia. Iran and Iraq move toward peace.

It is a watershed.

It is no accident.

It happened when we acted on the ancient knowledge that strength and clarity lead to peace – weakness and ambivalence lead to war. Weakness tempts aggressors. Strength stops them. I will not allow this country to be made weak again.

The tremors in the Soviet world continue. The hard earth there has not yet settled. Perhaps what is happening will change our world forever. Perhaps what is happening will change our world forever. Perhaps not. A prudent skepticism is in order. And so is hope. Either way, we're in an unprecedented position to change the nature of our relationship. Not by preemptive concession – but by keeping our strength. Not by yielding up defense systems with nothing won in return – but by hard cool engagement in the tug and pull of diplomacy.

My life has been lived in the shadow of war – I almost lost my life in one.

I hate war.

I love peace. We have peace.

And I am not going to let anyone take it away from us.

Our economy is strong but not invulnerable, and the peace is broad but can be broken. And now we must decide. We will surely have change this year, but will it be change that moves us forward? Or change that risks retreat?

In 1940, when I was barely more than a boy, Franklin Roosevelt said we shouldn't change horses in midstream.

My friends, these days the world moves even more quickly, and now, after two great terms, a switch will be made. But when you have to change horses in midstream, doesn't it make sense to switch to the one who's going the same way?

An election that is about ideas and values is also about philosophy. And I have one.

At the bright center is the individual. And radiating out from him or her is the family, the essential unit of closeness and of love. For it is the family that communicates to our children – to the 21st century – our culture, our religious faith, our traditions and history.

From the individual to the family to the community, and on out to the town, to the church and school, and, still echoing out, to the county, the state, the nation – each doing only what it does well, and no more. And I believe that power must always be kept close to the individual – close to the hands that raise the family and run the home.

I am guided by certain traditions. One is that there is a God and He is good, and his love, while free, has a self imposed cost: We must be good to one another.

I believe in another tradition that is, by now, embedded in the national soul. It is that learning is good in and of itself. The mothers of the Jewish ghettos of the east would pour honey on a book so the children would learn that learning is sweet. And the parents who settled hungry Kansas would take their children in from the fields when a teacher came. That is our history.

And there is another tradition. And that is the idea of community – a beautiful word with a big meaning. Though liberal democrats have an odd view of it. They see "community" as a limited cluster of interest groups, locked in odd conformity. In this view, the country waits passively while Washington sets the rules.

But that's not what community means — not to me.

For we are a nation of communities, of thousands and tens of thousands of ethnic, religious, social, business, labor union, neighborhood, regional and other organizations, all of them varied, voluntary and unique.

This is America: the Knights of Columbus, the Grange, Hadassah, the Disabled American Veterans, the Order of Ahepa, the Business and Professional Women of America, the union hall, the Bible study group, LULAC, "Holy Name" — a brilliant diversity spread like stars, like a thousand points of light in a broad and peaceful sky.

Does government have a place? Yes. Government is part of the nation of communities — not the whole, just a part.

I do not hate government. A government that remembers that the people are its master is a good and needed thing.

I respect old fashioned common sense, and have no great love for the imaginings of social planners. I like what's been tested and found to be true.

For instance:

Should public school teachers be required to lead our children in the pledge of allegiance? My opponent says no — but I say yes.

Should society be allowed to impose the death penalty on those who commit crimes of extraordinary cruelty and violence? My opponent says no — but I say yes.

Should our children have the right to say a voluntary prayer, or even observe a moment of silence in the schools? My opponent says no – but I say yes.

Should free men and women have the right to own a gun to protect their home? My opponent says no – but I say yes.

Is it right to believe in the sanctity of life and protect the lives of innocent children? My opponent says no – but I say yes. We must change from abortion – to adoption. I have an adopted granddaughter. The day of her christening we wept with joy. I thank God her parents chose life.

I'm the one who believes it is a scandal to give a weekend furlough to a hardened first degree killer who hasn't even served enough time to be eligible for parole.

I'm the one who says a drug dealer who is responsible for the death of a policeman should be subject to capital punishment.

I'm the one who won't raise taxes. My opponent now says he'll raise them as a last resort, or a third resort. When a politician talks like that, you know that's one resort he'll be checking into. My opponent won't rule out raising taxes. But I will. The Congress will push me to raise taxes, and I'll say no, and they'll push, and I'll say no, and they'll push again, and I'll say to them, *"Read my lips: no new taxes."*

Let me tell you more about the mission.

On jobs, my mission is: 30 in 8. Thirty million jobs in the next eight years.

Every one of our children deserves a first rate school. The liberal democrats want power in the hands of the federal government. I want power in the hands of parents. I will increase the power of parents. I will encourage merit schools. I will give more kids a Head Start. And I'll make it easier to save for college.

I want a drug free America – and this will not be easy to achieve. But I want to enlist the help of some people who are rarely included. Tonight I challenge the young people of our country to shut down the drug dealers around the world. Unite with us, work with us. "Zero tolerance" isn't just a policy, it's an attitude. Tell them what you think of people who underwrite the dealers who put poison in our society. And while you're doing that, my administration will be telling the dealers: whatever we have to do we'll do, but your day is over, you're history.

I am going to do whatever it takes to make sure the disabled are included in the mainstream. For too long they've been left out. But they're not going to be left out anymore.

I am going to stop ocean dumping. Our beaches should not be garbage dumps and our harbors should not be cesspools. I am going to have the FBI trace the medical wastes and we are going to punish the people who dump those infected needles into our oceans, lakes and rivers. And we must clean the air. We must reduce the harm done by acid rain.

I will put incentives back into the domestic energy industry, for I know from personal experience there is no security for the United States in further dependence on foreign oil.

In foreign affairs I will continue our policy of peace through strength. I will move toward further cuts in the strategic and conventional arsenals of both the United States and the Soviet Union. I will modernize and preserve our technological edge. I will ban chemical and biological weapons from the face of the earth. And I intend to speak for freedom, stand for freedom, and be a patient friend to anyone, east or west, who will fight for freedom.

It seems to me the Presidency provides an incomparable opportunity for "gentle persuasion."

I hope to stand for a new harmony, a greater tolerance. We've come far, but I think we need a new harmony among the races in our country. We're on a journey to a new century, and we've got to leave the tired old baggage of bigotry behind.

Some people who are enjoying our prosperity have forgotten what it's for. But they diminish our triumph when they act as if wealth is an end in itself.

There are those who have dropped their standards along the way, as if ethics were too heavy and slowed their rise to the top. There's graft in city hall, the greed on Wall Street; there's influence peddling in Washington, and the small corruptions of everyday ambition.

But you see, I believe public service is honorable. And every time I hear someone has breached the public trust it breaks my heart.

I wonder sometimes if we have forgotten who we are. But we're the people who sundered a nation rather than allow a sin called slavery — we're the people who rose from the ghettos and the deserts.

We weren't saints — but we lived by standards. We celebrated the individual — but we weren't self-centered. We were practical — but we didn't live only for material things. We believed in getting ahead — but blind ambition wasn't our way.

The fact is prosperity has a purpose. It is to allow us to pursue "the better angels," to give us time to think and grow. Prosperity with a purpose means taking your idealism and making it concrete by certain acts of goodness. It means helping a child from an unhappy home learn how to read – and I thank my wife Barbara for all her work in literacy. It means teaching troubled children through your presence that there's such a thing as reliable love. Some would say it's soft and insufficiently tough to care about these things. But where is it written that we must act as if we do not care, as if we are not moved?

Well I am moved. I want a kinder, gentler nation.

Two men this year ask for your support. And you must know us.

As for me, I have held high office and done the work of democracy day by day. My parents were prosperous; their children were lucky. But there were lessons we had to learn about life. John Kennedy discovered poverty when he campaigned in West Virginia; there were children there who had no milk. Young Teddy Roosevelt met the new America when he roamed the immigrant streets of New York. And I learned a few things about life in a place called Texas.

We moved to west Texas 40 years ago. The war was over, and we wanted to get out and make it on our own. Those were exciting days. We lived in a little shotgun house, one room for the three of us. Worked in the oil business, started my own.

In time we had six children. Moved from the shotgun to a duplex apartment to a house. Lived the dream – high school football on Friday night, Little League, neighborhood barbecue.

People don't see their experience as symbolic of an era – but of course we were. So was everyone else who was taking a chance and pushing into unknown territory with kids and a dog and a car. But the big thing I learned is the satisfaction of creating opportunity, which meant happy families, who in turn could do more to help others and enhance their own lives. I learned that the good done by a single good job can be felt in ways you can't imagine.

I may not be the most eloquent, but I learned early that eloquence won't draw oil from the ground. I may sometimes be a little awkward, but there's nothing self-conscious in my love of country. I am a quiet man but I hear the quiet people others don't. The ones who raise the family, pay the taxes, meet the mortgage. I hear them and I am moved, and their concerns are mine.

A President must be many things.

He must be a shrewd protector of America's interests; and he must be an idealist who leads those who move for a freer and more democratic planet.

He must see to it that government intrudes as little as possible in the lives of the people; and yet remember that it is the nation's character.

And he must be able to define – and lead – a mission.

For seven and a half years I have worked with a President – and I have seen what crosses that big desk. I have seen the unexpected crisis that arrives in a cable in a young aide's hand. And I have seen problems that simmer on for decades and suddenly demand resolution. I have seen modest decisions made with anguish, and crucial decisions made with dispatch.

And so I know that what it all comes down to, this election – what it all comes down to, after all the shouting and the cheers – is the man at the desk.

My friends, I am that man.

I say it without boast or bravado, I've fought for my country, I've served, I've built – and I will go from the hills to the hollows, from the cities to the suburbs to the loneliest town on the quietest street to take our message of hope and growth for every American to every American.

I will keep America moving forward, always forward – for a better America, for an endless enduring dream and a thousand points of light.

That is my mission. And I will complete it.

Thank you. God bless you.

Inaugural Address, January 20, 1989
West Front of the Capitol, Washington, D.C.

Mr. Chief Justice, Mr. President, Vice President Quayle, Senator Mitchell, Speaker Wright, Senator Dole, Congressman Michel, and fellow citizens, neighbors, and friends:

There is a man here who has earned a lasting place in our hearts and in our history. President Reagan, on behalf of our Nation, I thank you for the wonderful things that you have done for America.

I have just repeated word for word the oath taken by George Washington 200 years ago, and the Bible on which I placed my hand is the Bible on which he placed his. It is right that the memory of Washington be with us today, not only because this is our Bicentennial Inauguration, but because Washington remains the Father of our Country. And he would, I think, be gladdened by this day; for today is the concrete expression of a stunning fact: our continuity these 200 years since our government began.

We meet on democracy's front porch, a good place to talk as neighbors and as friends. For this is a day when our nation is made whole, when our differences, for a moment, are suspended.

And my first act as President is a prayer. I ask you to bow your heads:

> Heavenly Father, we bow our heads and thank You for Your love. Accept our thanks for the peace that yields this day and the shared faith that makes its continuance likely. Make us strong to do Your work, willing to heed and hear Your will, and write on our hearts these words: "Use power to help people." For we are given power not to advance our own purposes, nor to make a great show in the world, nor a name. There is but one just use of power, and it is to serve people. Help us to remember it, Lord. Amen.

I come before you and assume the Presidency at a moment rich with promise. We live in a peaceful, prosperous time, but we can make it better. For a new breeze is blowing, and a world refreshed by freedom seems reborn; for in man's heart, if not in fact, the day of the dictator is over. The totalitarian era is passing, its old ideas blown away like leaves from an ancient, lifeless tree. A new breeze is blowing, and a nation refreshed by freedom stands ready to push on. There is new ground to be broken, and new action to be taken. There are times when the future seems thick as a fog; you sit and wait, hoping the mists will lift and reveal the right path. But this is a time when the future seems a door you can walk right through into a room called tomorrow.

Great nations of the world are moving toward democracy through the door to freedom. Men and women of the world move toward free markets through the door to prosperity. The people of the world agitate for free expression and free thought through the door to the moral and intellectual satisfactions that only liberty allows.

We know what works: Freedom works. We know what's right: Freedom is right. We know how to secure a more just and prosperous life for man on Earth: through free markets, free speech, free elections, and the exercise of free will unhampered by the state.

For the first time in this century, for the first time in perhaps all history, man does not have to invent a system by which to live. We don't have to talk late into the night about which form of government is better. We don't have to wrest justice from the kings. We only have to summon it from within ourselves. We must act on what we know. I take as my guide the hope of a saint: In crucial things, unity; in important things, diversity; in all things, generosity.

America today is a proud, free nation, decent and civil, a place we cannot help but love. We know in our hearts, not loudly and proudly, but as a simple fact, that this country has meaning beyond what we see, and that our strength is a force for good. But have we changed as a nation even in our time? Are we enthralled with material things, less appreciative of the nobility of work and sacrifice?

My friends, we are not the sum of our possessions. They are not the measure of our lives. In our hearts we know what matters. We cannot hope only to leave our children a bigger car, a bigger bank account. We must hope to give them a sense of what it means to be a loyal friend, a loving parent, a citizen who leaves his home, his neighborhood and town better than he found it. What do we want the men and women who work with us to say when we are no longer there? That we were more driven to succeed than anyone around us? Or that we stopped to ask if a sick child had gotten better, and stayed a moment there to trade a word of friendship?

No President, no government, can teach us to remember what is best in what we are. But if the man you have chosen to lead this government can help make a difference; if he can celebrate the quieter, deeper successes that are made not of gold and silk, but of better hearts and finer souls; if he can do these things, then he must.

America is never wholly herself unless she is engaged in high moral principle. We as a people have such a purpose today. It is to make kinder the face of the Nation and gentler the face of the world. My friends, we have work to do. There are the homeless, lost and roaming. There are the children who have nothing, no love, no normalcy. There are those who cannot free themselves of enslavement to whatever addiction – drugs, welfare, the demoralization that rules the slums. There is crime to be conquered, the rough crime of the streets. There are young women to be helped who are about to become mothers of children they can't care for and might not love. They need our care, our guidance, and our education, though we bless them for choosing life.

The old solution, the old way, was to think that public money alone could end these problems. But we have learned that is not so. And in any case, our funds are low. We have a deficit to bring down. We have more will than wallet; but will is what we need. We will make the hard choices, looking at what we have and perhaps allocating it differently, making our decisions based on honest need and prudent safety. And then we will do the wisest thing of all: We will turn to the only resource we have that in times of need always grows – the goodness and the courage of the American people.

I am speaking of a new engagement in the lives of others, a new activism, hands-on and involved, that gets the job done. We must bring in the generations, harnessing the unused talent of the elderly and the unfocused energy of the young. For not only leadership is passed from generation to generation, but so is stewardship. And the generation born after the Second World War has come of age.

I have spoken of a thousand points of light, of all the community organizations that are spread like stars throughout the Nation, doing good. We will work hand in hand, encouraging, sometimes leading, sometimes being led, rewarding. We will work on this in the White House, in the

Cabinet agencies. I will go to the people and the programs that are the brighter points of light, and I will ask every member of my government to become involved. The old ideas are new again because they are not old; they are timeless: duty, sacrifice, commitment, and a patriotism that finds its expression in taking part and pitching in.

We need a new engagement, too, between the Executive and the Congress. The challenges before us will be thrashed out with the House and the Senate. We must bring the Federal budget into balance. And we must ensure that America stands before the world united, strong, at peace, and fiscally sound. But, of course, things may be difficult. We need compromise; we have had dissension. We need harmony; we have had a chorus of discordant voices.

For Congress, too, has changed in our time. There has grown a certain divisiveness. We have seen the hard looks and heard the statements in which not each other's ideas are challenged, but each other's motives. And our great parties have too often been far apart and untrusting of each other. It has been this way since Vietnam. That war cleaves us still. But, friends, that war began in earnest a quarter of a century ago; and surely the statute of limitations has been reached. This is a fact: The final lesson of Vietnam is that no great nation can long afford to be sundered by a memory. A new breeze is blowing, and the old bipartisanship must be made new again.

To my friends – and yes, I do mean friends – in the loyal opposition – and yes, I mean loyal: I put out my hand. I am putting out my hand to you, Mr. Speaker. I am putting out my hand to you, Mr. Majority Leader. For this is the thing: This is the age of the offered hand. We can't turn back clocks, and I don't want to. But when our fathers were young, Mr. Speaker, our differences ended at the water's edge. And we don't wish to turn back time, but when our mothers were young, Mr. Majority Leader, the Congress and the Executive were capable of working together to produce a budget on which this nation could live. Let us negotiate soon and hard. But in the end, let us produce. The American people await action. They didn't send us here to bicker. They ask us to rise above the merely partisan. "In crucial things, unity" – and this, my friends, is crucial.

To the world, too, we offer new engagement and a renewed vow: We will stay strong to protect the peace. The "offered hand" is a reluctant fist; but once made, strong, and can be used with great effect. There are today Americans who are held against their will in foreign lands, and Americans who are unaccounted for. Assistance can be shown here, and will be long remembered. Good will begets good will. Good faith can be a spiral that endlessly moves on.

Great nations like great men must keep their word. When America says something, America means it, whether a treaty or an agreement or a vow made on marble steps. We will always try to speak clearly, for candor is a compliment, but subtlety, too, is good and has its place. While keeping our alliances and friendships around the world strong, ever strong, we will continue the new closeness with the Soviet Union, consistent both with our security and with progress. One might say that our new relationship in part reflects the triumph of hope and strength over experience. But hope is good, and so are strength and vigilance.

Here today are tens of thousands of our citizens who feel the understandable satisfaction of those who have taken part in democracy and seen their hopes fulfilled. But my thoughts have been turning the past few days to those who would be watching at home, to an older fellow who will throw a salute by himself when the flag goes by, and the woman who will tell her sons the words of the battle hymns. I don't mean this to be sentimental. I mean that on days like this, we remember that we are all part of a continuum, inescapably connected by the ties that bind.

Our children are watching in schools throughout our great land. And to them I say, thank you for watching democracy's big day. For democracy belongs to us all, and freedom is like a beautiful kite that can go higher and higher with the breeze. And to all I say: No matter what your circumstances or where you are, you are part of this day, you are part of the life of our great nation.

A President is neither prince nor pope, and I don't seek a window on men's souls. In fact, I yearn for a greater tolerance, and easygoingness about each other's attitudes and way of life.

There are few clear areas in which we as a society must rise up united and express our intolerance. The most obvious now is drugs. And when that first cocaine was smuggled in on a ship, it may as well have been a deadly bacteria, so much has it hurt the body, the soul of our country. And there is much to be done and to be said, but take my word for it: This scourge will stop.

And so, there is much to do; and tomorrow the work begins. I do not mistrust the future; I do not fear what is ahead. For our problems are large, but our heart is larger. Our challenges are great, but our will is greater. And if our flaws are endless, God's love is truly boundless.

Some see leadership as high drama, and the sound of trumpets calling, and sometimes it is that. But I see history as a book with many pages, and each day we fill a page with acts of hopefulness and meaning. The new breeze blows, a page turns, the story unfolds. And so today a chapter begins, a small and stately story of unity, diversity, and generosity – shared, and written, together.

Thank you. God bless you and God bless the United States of America.

Statement on the Federal Budget Negotiations
June 26, 1990

I met this morning with the bipartisan leadership – the Speaker, the Senate majority leader, the Senate Republican leader, the House majority leader, and the House Republican leader – to review the status of the deficit reduction negotiations.

It is clear to me that both the size of the deficit problem and the need for a package that can be enacted require all of the following: entitlement and mandatory program reform, tax revenue increases, growth incentives, discretionary spending reductions, orderly reductions in defense expenditures, and budget process reform to assure that any bipartisan agreement is enforceable and that the deficit problem is brought under responsible control. The bipartisan leadership agree with me on these points.

The budget negotiations will resume promptly with a view toward reaching substantive agreement as quickly as possible.

Note: The statement referred to Thomas S. Foley, Speaker of the House of Representatives; George J. Mitchell, Senate majority leader; Richard A. Gephardt, House majority leader; and Robert H. Michel, House Republican leader.

Remarks Announcing A Federal Budget Agreement
September 30, 1990

The President. I am joined here today by the bipartisan leadership of the Congress-the Speaker of the House, the Senate majority leader, the Senate Republican leader, the President pro tem of the Senate, the House majority leader, and the House Republican leader – and other members of the budget summit negotiating group. The bipartisan leaders and I have reached agreement on the Federal budget. Over 5 years, it would reduce the projected deficit by $500 billion; that is half a trillion dollars.

The agreement has five basic parts. First, it would save $119 billion in entitlement and mandatory programs.

Second, it would produce $182 billion in discretionary program savings. These savings would come principally from defense. In the next 3 years, defense outlays would be reduced by $67 billion, relative to the projected baseline. All other discretionary programs would be firmly capped at the projected baseline levels; that is, for the next 3 years they would in total be allowed to grow at no more than the inflation rate.

Third, the agreement would increase tax revenues by $134 billion. The largest single increase, single contributor, would be a phased-in increase in the gasoline tax of 5 cents per gallon in the first year and another 5 cents in the following years. I do not welcome any such tax measure, nor do I expect anybody up here does. However, this one does have the virtue not only of contributing to deficit reduction but also, over time, of decreasing America's dependence on foreign oil, an objective whose importance has become increasingly evident in the face of the Iraqi invasion of Kuwait. I am pleased to be able to note that the budget agreement also includes several new incentives to increase domestic exploration and development of oil and gas resources. The combination of these measures should help reduce America's vulnerability to the interruption of supplies of foreign oil imports.

Fourth, the agreement extends the Gramm-Rudman budget discipline for 5 years. In addition, it improves the budget process and substantially strengthens the enforceability of the 5-year budget plan to which we have agreed.

Fifth, this agreement includes important new initiatives to stimulate economic growth: it authorizes new tax incentives for the development of enterprise zones; extends the R&D tax credit; it provides powerful new incentives for productive investment in the kinds of companies that account for most of America's job growth. These incentives include: a new 30-percent credit for R&D; 25-percent deduction for the purchase of new equity; indexing of the basis of new stock in such companies; expansion of expensing of investment in tangible equipment and scientific equipment; a minimum basis rule that encourages investment in new ventures and in companies with high growth potential; and other such incentives.

In addition to these targeted growth incentives I would note that prompt enactment of this entire 5-year deficit reduction package would itself help stimulate long-term economic growth with a half a trillion dollars in real deficit reduction. And let me repeat: The leaders here and I think that these are real deficit reduction figures. Long-term interest rates should be able to come down.

This package should be a strong component of a positive, responsible fiscal and monetary policy. I heartily thank the negotiators who have worked so long and so hard to develop this package. The bipartisan congressional leadership and I have pledged our very best to get this entire package signed into law by October 19th. As any such plan would have to, ours requires that virtually everyone contribute in some way. It is balanced, it is fair, and in my view it is what the United States of America needs at this point in its history. And we are united in our firm determination to see this program enacted.

I do not want to imply that some who have not been in the final negotiations are for every part of this. But I can only speak for my part, and then the top leadership here will speak. But I will simply say: This is priority. This is priority for our nation. This is something that the country is calling out for and world markets are looking for. And so, there will be some tough fights ahead; but I have pledged to the Speaker, to Congressman Gephardt, to Bob Michel on our side, to George Mitchell and Bob Dole and the Senate pro tem leader, Senator Byrd, that I will do everything I can to lay aside partisanship here and to take the case for this deal to the American people in every way I can. *Sometimes you don't get it just the way you want, and this is such a time for me, and I expect it's such a time for everybody standing here. But it's time we put the interest of the United States of America first and get this deficit under control.*

Mr. Speaker, I am grateful to you, the Democrats, and the Republicans that have seen that the interest of this country come first. Thank you for what you've been doing, and I'd appreciate it if you want to say a few words.

Speaker Foley. Thank you very much, Mr. President. I'll be brief in just echoing what you, yourself, just said, sir, that this is a package that your negotiators and the bipartisan participating negotiators from the House and the Senate – ranking Republican Members, chairmen, and the leadership on both sides – have sought to achieve. It's not going to be easy or simple to obtain the votes that are necessary in both the House and the Senate, the majority of both parties and both bodies, that will have to be found to enact this package – and within the next 3 weeks. But we pledge our efforts with yours to convince our colleagues in the country that this is a strong undergirding of our economic future, our national prosperity, and joint national interest. And in that spirit, we are going to begin today to present to you legislation which will allow the orderly functioning of the Federal Government for the continuation of this next week, in preparing to take the first step to implement this program.

I want to pay a word, if I can, of special thanks to all of my colleagues who have participated in this, and especially to Dick Gephardt, the chairman of these budget negotiations, who, all sides – Republicans and Democrats, Senators and House Members, and you, yourself – have spoken eloquently to his patience and leadership. Thank you, sir, for your involvement and your determination to aid in the process of bringing this package and the interests of the country to final achievement.

The President. Now if I might ask Senator Mitchell and then Senator Dole, Congressman Gephardt, and Congressman Michel to speak.

Senator Mitchell. Thank you, Mr. President. Now comes the hard part. It's one thing to get a budget agreement among ourselves for which all involved should be commended. It's another thing to get the votes to pass it through the House and the Senate. That is a task to which we must now commit ourselves.

This agreement is a compromise. Both sides can accurately say that the agreement includes provisions they don't like. Both sides can also accurately say the agreement doesn't include some provisions they think should be included. Cutting the deficit requires difficult choices. But our nation's economic future requires that we make those choices. We have already debated too long. Now we must act decisively.

Senator Dole. Mr. President, thank you very much. And I want to thank my colleagues and again, particularly Dick Gephardt. The nay-sayers and the nitpickers may have a field day because the easy vote in this case is to find something you don't like and vote no. But in my view, we owe more to the American people than finding fault with what I consider to be a good, positive, solid agreement that, in my view, will help the American economy and demonstrate to the American people, who are sometimes somewhat cynical, that the Congress and the President of the United States can work together, and we can look ahead and we can do the right thing for our country. And so, I would hope that my colleagues – and I speak now to my colleagues – certainly will study this document very carefully, will give it their best effort, and when the role is called that we'll have a majority of Republicans and Democrats for this outstanding package.

Thank you, Mr. President.

The President. Thank you. Dick?

Representative Gephardt. Thank you, Mr. President. Forty years ago a mountaineer who joined in the first successful climb of Mount Everest explained the success by saying no expedition enjoyed better teamwork. To the Speaker of the House, Congressman Foley; the Senate majority leader, George Mitchell; to the Members of Congress who are here with us on the stage; to the administration and their representatives and the great staffs of all sides who worked so long and so hard with us: You have been heroic as we've made this climb together.

The American people are today asking: Why was this summit necessary, why did it take so long, and what did it achieve? If we are to enact this agreement — and I think we must — these questions must be answered persuasively and honestly. For 10 years we have chosen a course together that has created large deficits and limited our capacity to meet the needs of our people and the demands of a very challenging age. Today, we face a weakened economy and high rates of interest and inflation. Tomorrow, in absence of an agreement, massive across-the-board budget cuts would occur.

The alternative to this agreement is fiscal chaos. To meet our responsibility to America's working families, this summit simply had to succeed. What delayed us for months is what has divided us for a decade. The parties to these talks had — and continue to have — deep disagreements over values, the role of government, and the fairness of our taxes. But we all made compromise in the national interest.

To bring this process to a successful conclusion, all of us — the American people and our national leaders — must accept the responsibilities of the day. And as this debate unfolds I hope this will be said: that we achieved the largest deficit reduction package in our history, that we focused the national debate on whether the tax code will be based on everybody's individual ability to pay. The vital issues — investing in our people, making our nation competitive, and realizing social justice — will rise again on the national agenda, and then enactment of this measure will enable us to confront these important issues successfully in the years to come.

I thank you, Mr. President, and I thank all the members of the summit.

The President. Bob?

Representative Michel. Well, thank you, Mr. President, and my colleagues. I support the package wholeheartedly because I was one of the narrower group that, within the last 10 days or so, made some of the final decisions.

There may be some reservations with respect to some of our other summiteers on the platform. I think probably rightly so because we're making decisions that will reach far out, to 5 years. Everyone is entitled to know exactly what we have wrought in the printed word. As a matter of fact, I wasn't privy to the last few lines that were written early this morning.

But, on balance, when I look at what we were originally faced with – and here we are refraining from increasing marginal rates and not touching the unmentionable out there, Social Security – and then to have the incentives for growth that I see here and the expenditure caps over the next several years that are real and enforceable, it seems to me that in the alternative so much better that we've done what we've done, and hopefully that in the ensuing days we'll be able to sell a majority of the Members on both sides of the aisle in both Houses to give us the affirmative vote that I think is so imperative that we have before we adjourn.

Thank you, Mr. President.

The President. Well, thank you all very much. And let me conclude by singling out the White House team by name: Secretary Brady and Dick Darman, John Sununu, who stayed in there day in and day out with the Members of Congress. In my view they did an outstanding job, too.

You know, Senator Bentsen said in this meeting – I hope it's not betraying a confidence – that he hoped that I would do my level-best to take this case to the American people. And I told him inside what I want to repeat here: I will do everything I can to generate support from the American people for this compromise.

I am convinced that the American people do not want to see us continue to mortgage the futures of their children and their grandchildren. And as I say, compromise is the word here. All of us have had to do that. But to Senator Bentsen I said in there, and I would say it here publicly: I want the American people to understand how important we feel this is. I want them to understand this is real. It is not a phony smoke-and-mirrors deficit-cutting program. And I will do everything in my power to help the leadership, Republican and Democrat, get this passed in the United States Congress.

The President. Thank you all very much for coming.

Remarks on Signing a Resolution Providing Funding for Continued Government Operation and a Question-and-Answer Session With Reporters in New York, New York
October 1, 1990

The President. The bill that I'm signing here today will keep the Government operating through October 5th, pending passage by Congress of a budget resolution which reflects the summit agreement. It also provides the important supplemental funds for Operation Desert Shield.

This bill represents the first step in implementing the budget summit agreement. And now it's up to Congress. The budget agreement we've reached is a good package. This budget is the right package at the right time. It is important to our nation. And it represents our best chance to get the deficit under control.

To the American people, I would say this agreement is balanced, it is fair, and it is absolutely critical to our country that we get an agreement through the Congress. We cannot keep mortgaging the futures of our children and our grandchildren, and we will not.

To the Congress, I would say that this is a time for leadership. We must put aside partisanship for the sake of our nation. We must act now to solve this budget problem.

I would also say this to Congress: Many of us in the political leadership have spoken for years about the need to deal with the deficit. As is usually the case in politics, many different approaches have been urged. We now have a deficit reduction package. It is a good package. It is a compromise. Certainly, I didn't get everything I wanted, and the Democrat leadership didn't get everything they wanted. But like most compromises, it's certainly not going to satisfy everyone. But this is the time to move beyond these individual concerns and exercise leadership for the good of the country.

The deficit reduction package is a balanced package. It cuts spending. It provides incentives for jobs and economic growth. It cleans up the budget-process mess. And it raises needed revenues without raising personal tax rates. And most important, these deficit measures are real; they have real teeth. It's time to end the talk about the deficit. It is time for action on the deficit. And it's time – I think past time – to put the interest of the country first.

And so, I will now sign this joint resolution and keep things moving.

{At this point, the President signed the resolution.}

I'd be glad to take a couple of questions on this or any other subject before I go on – at the United Nations. It's been a busy one, and I'll be glad to take a few, and then have to go.

Federal Budget Agreement

Q. Is there a planned attack to sell those conservative Republicans, who are already saying they're not going to vote for this?

The President. Well, I want to sell the Democrats who are saying they won't vote for it, and I want to sell the Republicans who are saying they won't – absolutely. When I go back, I'll do my best. I'll take the case, as I'm doing to some degree here, to the American people. I've already been on the telephone. And I think back to what President Reagan had to do in the early eighties. And I heard the hue and cry from Democrats and Republicans, and I could understand it. I mean, if I were in the Congress, maybe I'd be screaming about something I wanted the most. But the time for this has passed. This is too serious now. And the leadership have worked hard. And so, you bet I'll be selling to everybody I can get to listen to me.

Q. But does it concern you, sir, that the loudest voices come from within your own party –

The President. I don't think –

Q. – especially on the issue of taxes?

The President. I don't think it's the loudest. Depends who you – I was watching on the tube last night, and I put down a few of the Democrats as unenthused. But look, expect that. What you've got to do is explain the country's at stake here, and that's what I plan to do.

Persian Gulf Crisis

Q. Mr. President, your speech today is being interpreted as having a little bit of a conciliatory tone. And you also brought in the Arab-Israeli conflict that would seem to be along Mitterrand's [President of France] pattern. Is there something new you were offering?

The President. No.

Q. Is there some sort of an olive branch in all of this that —

The President. No.

Q. What do you mean, no?

The President. I mean, no, there's no change in my position.

Q. But you did offer negotiations, and you seem to be holding out —

The President. Let me — I thought I might get this question, so I've underlined it in this yellow pen here. *{Laughter}* "In the aftermath of Iraq's unconditional departure from Kuwait, there may be opportunities." Now, unconditional is what the United Nations is calling for, and that's what the United States — so there's no flexibility here. And I was surprised when I heard that some were interpreting it as such.

We've got to keep together. The thing that I've garnered through many, many talks up here is almost that — well, it's totally solid support for the U.N. position and the U.S. position. So, there isn't flexibility. And I'm glad to get a chance to clear that up.

Q. But you don't think there's solid support for military action, do you?

The President. I don't know. As I've said, I want to see a peaceful resolution if at all possible. We'll cross that bridge when we get to it. But I have heard rather encouraging words on two points: one, that Saddam Hussein [President of Iraq] is beginning to understand that it is he against the world; and secondly, there's more optimism in various quarters that the sanctions are really beginning to bite hard.

So, both of those have been reinforced for me. And so, we'll just have to wait and see. But this was not designed to convey flexibility or shift in position.

Q. But, Mr. President, your words were that after this unconditional withdrawal there may be opportunities for Iraq and Kuwait to settle their differences permanently. We were told, you were told last week by the Amir [Amir Jabir al-Ahmad al-Jabir Al Sabah of Kuwait] that Kuwait is being dismantled by Iraq.

The President. They are, and that's why they have to get out now.

Q. They're taking away everything that can be moved. Are you suggesting that perhaps Iraq can get those disputed islands if they pull out now?

The President. No.

Q. What are you suggesting?

The President. No, let me be very clear. I'm just suggesting that you've got to make whole Kuwait the way it was – and absolutely not that there can be any giving away by the United States or the United Nations of anything. The restoration of Kuwait, its leaders, is a terribly important part of this. They should go back there. And Iraq should unilaterally and unconditionally withdraw.

Q. And if I could follow: You mentioned today the eight major resolutions. Do you want a ninth major resolution clearly stating that the U.N. multilateral force is authorized to go in and do combat with Iraq?

The President. We have not been pressing for that at this point. You heard Prime Minister Thatcher [of the United Kingdom] on that, I guess, this morning. But we're still pursuing the road that let's get these sanctions to work, let's get the forces in place. And let's hope that the little optimism I'm picking up around here about the sanctions will prevail.

There's also another theme that this man, if you look at his record, will do a 180. You look at the history with Iran, and he's done a 180-degree turn and done exactly what he said he wouldn't do. So, some people are basing their hopes on that, some of the diplomats I've talked to.

Q. Mr. President, you don't come to the United Nations very often, and certainly, you were trying to emphasize something here that you haven't said in the past. I wondered what it might have been, if anything.

The President. Now, Saul [Saul Friedman, Newsday], why would you say I would want to emphasize something? I want to keep emphasizing what I have been saying in the past, and that is that the United Nations has done a superb job. These resolutions are unprecedented. We have the broadest possible support to stand up against this aggression, and we want to see the unilateral withdrawal, unconditional withdrawal from Kuwait. It's a question of emphasis, but I'm not trying to convey something new in that. I know you're a foreign affairs – you love the nuance. [Laughter] But seriously, you're reading too much into this. There's not any nuance to this that you think you might be missing.

Q. Do you agree with Mrs. Thatcher, who also said on television this morning that the United States or the allies would not need any further permission from the United Nations in the use of military force?

The President. Well, we felt that under article 51 that authorization was there. And I think she was talking about 51. However, you may remember that we waited until we got a resolution before interdicting ships that more directly confirmed the right to do that. But, no, I agree with her on that point.

Q. Mr. President, given the brutality of the Iraqi occupation and their efforts to develop the germ warfare capability, how long can we afford to wait for Saddam to do a 180?

The President. Well, it's a very good question to which I don't have the answer; I don't know the answer to that question. And it goes back to this question about what the Amir told me about the dismantling, rape, pillage, and plunder of that country. So, I can't put a time frame on that for you. I wish I had a clearer answer for the American people. I don't.

Q. Mr. President, do you believe that Saddam Hussein is capable of a 180 at this point? And if he does pull a 180, doesn't that still leave him as an irritant in the region, a major military threat?

The President. The answer is: I'm just taking on board what I've been told by people that have studied it carefully – that he is capable of that. I should tell you this, though. That's the one hand. On the other hand, there are those who say that if he withdraws from Kuwait that is the end of him because of having had to withdraw from Iran. So, you have to weigh the two.

But I don't have to act on these opinions. I have to just keep this consensus together; keep getting the sanctions as tight as possible; and hope that that makes him understand that, alone against the rest of the world, he has to do what the United Nations called for.

What was the second part, Mick [Jim Miklaszewski, NBC News]?

Q. Well, doesn't that leave him – a 180 – wouldn't that leave him an irritant, a potential military threat in the area?

The President. You mean just if he went back to the status quo ante? Yes, it would be a problem, and it would have to be resolved in some way.

Q. If I may follow up —

The President. That's the third followup. Go ahead. What's the second followup?

Q. Was that your reference to chemical weapons in today's speech? In other words, after Iraq pulls out of Kuwait, if that happens, was that what you were referring to in terms of eliminating chemical weapons in the region?

The President. No, I wasn't specifically referring to that. But this is a very troublesome capability he has, and it does worry us. But I think there would be great unease about the simple status quo ante. But we've been talking here about the dismantling of Kuwait. I'm sure there would be claims in that regard. The international community would have to have something to say about that. I'm sure that neighbors would want to know that there was not a risk of another reckless invasion of this nature. And then that would lead you to say, well, what kind of security provisions would be put into effect?

So, it's not a clear withdrawal to the status quo ante that would solve everything, but it is what's called for under these resolutions.

Federal Budget Agreement

Q. This budget agreement that you have Mr. President, is it one that's likely to look better in '92 when you're running for re-election than it does to Republicans now?

The President. I think what matters at this juncture is not who's running in the fall of '90 and not who's running in the fall in '92 but what's best for the country in the fall of 1990, what is essential for the country. And I think getting this deficit down with a realistic program is essential for our country.

I've said – and I'm not looking at this in a political way – we've got to get it done. I've had to compromise; the Democrats have had to compromise. And I hope that other voices who are troubled by one aspect or another of this or something that wasn't in it that they wanted would also compromise. Every once in a while, you come to a position, come to a time, when you have to do that to get something done.

I don't control the Congress. I don't control either House of the Congress as the President. My party doesn't control it. But I was elected to govern. And I can stand; I can veto; I can do a lot of things. But the time, in my view, has come, because of the seriousness of the deficit, to lay aside getting it done exactly the way I want; to make a compromise, which I think is a good one, to preserve many of the things I want; and to go forward and get it put into effect.

So, it's in that spirit and not in the spirit of elections. And I would refer those on either side who worry about their election to look at the debate around the two tax increases that President Reagan had to go forward with. And there wasn't a political fallout because I think the country understands when the President concludes that a deal is necessary, they're inclined to give him the benefit of the doubt.

Q. What then does it say about campaign promises, such as "cut capital gains tax" and "read my lips"?

The President. It says you need more Republicans, and then we'll do it exactly my way. But we don't have that right now, so you have to do the best you can, Charles [Charles Bierbauer, Cable News Network]. It's funny, but that's the way it works. I'll be glad to take my case out there. I'll say: If you want all these things, give me some more Republicans. That comes after we get a deal. And then we go right through the election cycle again. I've tried that.

We don't control the Congress. They're not going to do it exactly my way. So, I've had to compromise, and the Republican leadership has compromised, and so have the Democrat leaders. So, I'm not about to start flailing away on that. I want this deal through. It would be unproductive to start unleashing a fall of '90 campaign during these critical days here.

Q. You haven't broken your promises?

The President. I'm not interested in talking about that. I'm interested in governing. But let me tell you this. I expect others will be talking about that. Fine. Take the heat, take the hit. There have been changed times. It didn't work the way I want. I don't have the horses in the Congress to do it exactly my way. So you have to govern, you have to lead, and that's what I'm trying to do.

Persian Gulf Crisis

Q. You say you are not pressing for an additional sanction now for military action. Is it because you don't have support for that kind –

The President. No, because we're still giving sanctions the time to work, the time to be effective. And I'm a little encouraged that perhaps they are having a strong effect. But so, we're not pressing for that right now.

Federal Budget Agreement

Q. When you made the big concessions, sir, especially on taxes and on capital gains, how motivated were you at that point about the fear of recession?

The President. I've been concerned about the fear of a recession. I'm concerned about a slow economy. And I believe a good budget agreement will result in lower interest rates. I would look to the Federal Reserve to lower the rates. I hope they would once they see that a sound budget agreement has been put into effect. And I would hope they think this is a sound budget agreement. *So, I am concerned, but I don't want to talk ourselves into recession. The President has to be very careful in commenting on prices, on markets.* But I believe — and I must say the initial market response just today — I don't know how it's going to play out over the days — has been rather encouraging, saying, well, markets are looking for a deal.

Q. I'm going to ask you a long question so the camera has time to put in fresh videotape because I think we've run out.

The President. You want me to come back?

Persian Gulf Crisis

Q. Are you more optimistic, sir, after the 21 or 22 one-on-ones [bilateral meetings held in New York City] or whatever it is?

The President. On the Middle East?

Q. On the Persian Gulf.

The President. Well, what I'm optimistic about is that there isn't one single breach in the armor. I didn't hear one single voice.

And I haven't listened to all the speeches, but some respected diplomats over there tell me nobody rose to the podium to defend Saddam Hussein. They said they've never seen it quite this united on any question of any kind. And let's hope then that he'll understand that he stands alone. And let's hope that that, coupled with the economic sanctions, will cause him to do what he's done in the past: do a 180 and get out.

Federal Budget Agreement

Q. Speaking of a breach, Mr. President, what about Newt [Representative Newt Gingrich]?

The President. I just told you, I understand the Republicans that don't like certain aspects of this deal. I understand Democrats that don't like certain aspects of this deal. And I'm going to be encouraging all those Republicans and all those Democrats to vote for it. And I don't like some aspects of it, and I don't expect George Mitchell and Tom Foley do, or Bob Dole and Bob Michel. Every once in a while in your country's history you've got to lay aside what you feel the most strongly about and come together. And I'm going to urge as many Democrats and Republicans as possible to come together.

Q. But wouldn't you at least expect one of the Republican budget negotiators to support the package?

The President. I'd expect all Republicans and all Democrats to support me, but that's not the way it works in real life.

I'd like to raffle – [laughter]. No –

Q. What happened to Gingrich and [Senator] Packwood?

Bill-Signing Pen

The President. Helen [Helen Thomas, United Press International], you be the start here. Are you the senior representative of the press corps?

Q. Yes.

The President. You get the pen that shows the signing of — would you like this memorialized —

Q. Great. A 5-day pen. *{Laughter}*

The President. Thank you. This counts on Marlin's books as a full press conference, the equivalent of an East Room press conference. He said if I made it for 10 minutes that we'd rack it up as the 71st. As long as we've survived for 25, it's the equivalent of one of those that we used to do with everybody all dressed up, you know. *{Laughter}*

Trip to Saudi Arabia

Q. Are you going to Saudi Arabia?

The President. *Hey, listen, I'm tired. I've got to go. What?*

Q. Are you going to Saudi Arabia for Thanksgiving?

The President. Not set, not settled. I've been reading in the paper that I'm going.

Address to the Nation

Q. — — about the budget? Do you think that's needed?

The President. Not set yet, but if it would help, I would be glad to do it. In fact, some of the Democrats raised that and others too, some of the Republicans. I'm going to get home now, and then we'll try to figure out what's the best way to get this message across.

Note: The President spoke at 2:07 p.m. at the Waldorf-Astoria Hotel. In his remarks, he referred to George J. Mitchell, Senate majority leader; Thomas S. Foley, Speaker of the House of Representatives; Robert Dole, Senate minority leader; and Robert H. Michel, Republican leader in the House of Representatives. Marlin Fitzwater is Press Secretary to the President. H.J. Res. 655, approved October 1, was assigned Public Law No. 101-403.

Remarks to Business Leaders
on the Federal Budget Agreement
October 2, 1990

Thank you very, very much for coming over. I met this morning with the Republican Members of the Congress to underscore the necessity for quick and decisive action on the budget agreement through the bipartisan leadership in both Houses. And I again am calling on the Congress to act, and act soon, on this vital legislation. Tonight I'm going to take the case for this budget agreement to the American people on a national television address at 9 p.m.

But to you all I want to say I appreciate the past support. I know that there are provisions in this that cause different people different problems, and I understand all that. And I will say, in achieving this agreement, everybody has had to compromise. *I did it because the country, frankly, is at stake here. And every once in a while in one's Presidency, I think it dawns on the incumbent of the Oval Office that you're not going to get it exactly your own way.* In this case, my party does not control both Houses of the Congress. But *as I look at the ever-increasing deficits, I think it is time we do something and do something serious.*

And with that philosophy has emerged this budget agreement. And I don't want to sound sanctimonious about this, but I was elected to govern. I was elected to make things happen. And we're trying to do that in the international scene, and where now it's time to come and do something on the domestic scene that will benefit all Americans.

I think — respecting the differences that do exist not only in this room but in the Congress — I think we all realize the time has come to get America's fiscal house in order. And I honestly believe — and this is what I came over to tell you — that this compromise is a major step towards this goal. By 1955 [1995] it will bring government spending as a percentage of gross national product to its lowest level since 1966.

And let me tell you what the budget agreement will do. Overview: The 5-year bipartisan budget compromise will boost our economic vitality in the long run. It will give small-and medium-sized business a shot in the arm and create jobs. It will reduce the deficit by $500 billion, the single biggest cut ever agreed to, and that is the prerequisite for bringing real interest rates down. I believe firmly that if we get this agreement through without watering it down that interest rates will come down.

The budget agreement raises the prospect of a long-term healthy economy. It raises the potential for growth. It raises America's ability to compete. But it does not raise personal income tax rates. I was able, with the help of the negotiators — or put it this way: They did all the heavy lifting on it but held the line on tax rates, which is something that I feel strongly about.

On the growth incentive side, the agreement includes incentives for oil and gas development. If there ever was a time when we needed to become less dependent on foreign oil, it's now, and I think these incentives can help in that direction. Incentives for the development of enterprise zones to create jobs and opportunity and, specifically, to keep small business competitive.

So, there are small business incentives that I'd like to ask you to look at very carefully: a 30-percent research and experimentation credit, tax indexing for individuals who buy stock in small corporations, a tax deduction for investment in small corporations, and an expanded ability for small businesses to expense certain scientific equipment.

On the domestic cuts – and here I think everybody in this room, whether you agree with me or not, knows that I wanted to get a capital gains cut. I also wanted to hold the line on tax rates. We're half successful, but we have some incentives here that I think will accomplish some of what I had in mind when I spoke about the growth in jobs and opportunity that would come from capital gains. So, look hard at these incentives.

Domestic cuts: The agreement will cut the projected Federal deficit by half a trillion dollars, with nearly $120 billion in real and enforceable spending cuts on entitlement and mandatory programs. And I'll ask – John and the others here are well equipped to give you details on this. But we feel these are real and enforceable spending cuts, and they do have teeth. For the first time, they will be guaranteed in law. No smoke or mirrors in this category here.

Now, let me just say, if we do not reform entitlements to bring their growth under control, as this agreement does, we'll never be able to solve the whole problem of the deficit. America's going to be unable to invest in the future because the entire budget would be gobbled up by entitlements and also interest on this ever-increasing debt.

On military cuts: Although the defense budget is cut by $67 billion over 3 years, and then more over 5, the Persian Gulf forces will still get the backing that they deserve to accomplish their mission. And frankly, I am one who happens to believe we need a strong defense and have always supported defense spending.

I think everyone in this room is realistic in that defense was going to take a hit, but it comes out better than I thought it would. And of course, this is causing strains on some who disagree as to whether we ought to have a strong defense spending or not. But here's one where these negotiators have done an extraordinarily good job.

On budget reform: The budget discipline of Gramm-Rudman will be extended for 5 years, and the agreement includes substantial budget-process reform. Once again, I didn't get everything I wanted. I've gone around calling for a line-item veto. That one never got out of the chutes, frankly. But I still would like to have it. It's not part of it, but we do have some substantial budget-process reform.

Now, if Congress spends the money it doesn't have, then a minisequester will come into effect and will cut it for them. So, for the next 5 years, all discretionary spending by Congress is capped.

And for the first time, mandatory entitlements, which have been the biggest source of spending growth, will be subject to a sequester to keep their growth under control. New entitlements will be subject to a pay-as-you-go system: they can't grow without offsetting cuts or revenues to cover their cost.

The budget is tough; it really is. It is fair, and again, it really is. It is a solid package to boost economic growth and solve long-term problems without having the burden fall entirely on any one group. The time has come to move beyond the narrow interests and put the broad interests of the United States first.

Most importantly, this budget agreement is our last, best chance to get the Federal budget deficit under control. To all the people that disagree and the people on the sidelines that are rushing out and having their press conferences and the critics, let me say this: You can pick the package apart, but you cannot realistically put a better package together.

Again, the philosophy that I was elected on runs out of gas in terms of votes in the United States Congress. And I think everybody here – and I've had enormous support for the various men and women in this room, strong support, who support me on difficult calls on veto overrides. But to get something done, to have something positive happen and have it happen in anything like timely fashion, I will say once again, there's been some compromise here. But we've tried in many ways, through single pieces of legislation, to get some of my philosophical underpinning for the economy put into effect. And we've tried hard, with the help, as I say, of people here. And we've simply failed because the votes aren't there. But here's a package that I think preserves much of what I believe. I've had to give some. We've taken some. And I just came over to strongly urge your support.

I'm grateful to the Vice President for his advocacy of this program up on the Hill. He did a superb job yesterday. I want to give a vote of confidence to all sitting up at the head table here – the dais or whatever we call it – who worked so hard on this. But John Sununu and Nick Brady and Dick Darman spent endless hours, endless hours, trying to hammer out the best possible deal; and I think they've done exactly that.

So, it has my enthusiastic support. Again I would like those who have reservations to look hard at it, to study it, to consider the fact that alternatives have been tried and we weren't able to get them through. And then I would like to ask your strong support for this package. The country is at stake here, and we need you. We need you bad.

So, thank you all very much. And now for the experts. Thank you.

Note: The President spoke at 1:16 p.m. in Room 450 of the Old Executive Office Building. In his remarks, he referred to John H. Sununu, Chief of Staff to the President; Secretary of the Treasury Nicholas F. Brady; and Richard G. Darman, Director of the Office of Management and Budget.

Address to the Nation on the
Federal Budget Agreement
October 2, 1990

Tonight I want to talk to you about a problem that has lingered and dogged and vexed this country for far too long: the Federal budget deficit. Thomas Paine said many years ago, "These are the times that try men's souls." As we speak, our nation is standing together against Saddam Hussein's aggression. But here at home there's another threat, a cancer gnawing away at our nation's health. That cancer is the budget deficit.

Year after year, it mortgages the future of our children. No family, no nation can continue to do business the way the Federal Government has been operating and survive. When you get a bill, that bill must be paid. And when you write a check, you're supposed to have money in the bank. But if you don't obey these simple rules of common sense, there's a price to pay.

But for too long, the Nation's business in Washington has been conducted as if these basic rules did not apply. Well, these rules do apply. And if we fail to act, next year alone we will face a Federal budget deficit of *more than $300 billion, a deficit that could weaken our economy further and cost us thousands of precious jobs. If what goes up must come down, then the way down could be very hard.*

But it doesn't have to be that way. We can do something. In fact, we have started to do something. But we must act this week, when Congress will hold the first of two crucial up-or-down votes. These votes will be on a deficit reduction agreement worked out between the administration and the bipartisan leaders of Congress. This budget agreement is the result of 8 months of blood, sweat, and fears – fears of the economic chaos that would follow if we fail to reduce the deficit.

Of course, I cannot claim it's the best deficit reduction plan possible. It's not. Any one of us alone might have written a better plan. But it is the best agreement that can be legislated now. It is the biggest deficit reduction agreement ever – half a trillion dollars. It's the toughest deficit reduction package ever, with new enforcement rules to make sure that what we fix now stays fixed. And it has the largest spending savings ever – more than $300 billion. *For the first time, a Republican President and leaders of a Democratic Congress have agreed to real cuts that will be enforced by law, not promises – no smoke, no mirrors, no magic act, but real and lasting spending cuts.*

This agreement will also raise revenue. I'm not, and I know you're not, a fan of tax increases. But if there have to be tax measures, they should allow the economy to grow, they should not turn us back to higher income tax rates, and they should be fair. Everyone who can should contribute something, and no one should have to contribute beyond their fair share. Our bipartisan agreement meets these tests. And through specific new incentives, it will help create more jobs.

It's a little-known fact, but America's best job creators and greatest innovators tend to be our smaller companies. So, our budget plan will give small and medium-size companies a needed shot in the arm. Just as important, I am convinced that this agreement will help lower interest rates. And lower interest rates mean savings for consumers, lower mortgage payments for new homeowners, and more investment to produce more jobs. And that's what this agreement will do.

Now, let me tell you what this agreement will not do. It will not raise income tax rates, personal or corporate. It will not mess with Social Security in any way. It will not put America's national security at risk. And most of all, it will not let our economy slip out of control.

Clearly, each and every one of us can find fault with something in this agreement. In fact, that is a burden that any truly fair solution must carry. Any workable solution must be judged as a whole, not piece by piece. Those who dislike one part or another may pick our agreement apart. But if they do, believe me, the political reality is, no one can put a better one back together again. Everyone will bear a small burden. But if we succeed, every American will have a large burden lifted. If we fail to enact this agreement, our economy will falter, markets may tumble, and recession will follow.

In just a moment, the Democratic majority leader, Senator Mitchell, will offer what is known as the Democratic response, often a rebuttal. But not tonight. Tonight the Democratic and Republican leadership and I all speak with one voice in support of this agreement. Tonight we ask you to help us move this agreement forward. The congressional leadership and I both have a job to do in getting it enacted. And tonight I ask for your help.

First, I ask you to understand how important — and for some, how difficult — this vote is for your Congressmen and Senators. Many worry about your reaction to one part or another. But I know you know the importance of the whole. And so, second, I ask you to take this initiative: Tell your Congressmen and Senators you support this deficit reduction agreement. If they are Republicans, urge them to stand with the President. Urge them to do what the bipartisan leadership has done: come together in the spirit of compromise to solve this national problem. If they're Democrats, urge them to stand with their congressional leaders. Ask them to fight for the future of your kids by supporting this budget agreement.

Now is the time for you, the American people, to have a real impact. Your Senators and Congressmen need to know that you want this deficit brought down, that the time for politics and posturing is over, and the time to come together is now.

This deficit reduction agreement is tough, and so are the times. The agreement is fair, and so is the American spirit. The agreement is bipartisan, and so is the vote. The agreement is real, and so is this crisis.

This is the first time in my Presidency that I've made an appeal like this to you, the American people. With your help, we can at last put this budget crisis behind us and face the other challenges that lie ahead. If we do, the long-term result will be a healthier nation and something more: We will have once again put ourselves on the path of economic growth, and we will have demonstrated that no challenge is greater than the determination of the American people.

Thank you. God bless you, and good night.

Note: The President spoke at 9 p.m. from the Oval Office at the White House. In his address, he referred to President Saddam Hussein of Iraq. The address was broadcast live on nationwide radio and television.

The President's News Conference
on the Federal Budget Crisis
October 6, 1990

The President. I just wanted to comment. I know the leaders have been speaking. And I have not yet signed but, within the next couple of minutes, will veto the continuing resolution. We've had good cooperation from the Democrat and Republican leaders. The Congress has got to get on with the people's business. I'd like them to do that business – get a budget resolution – and get it done in the next 24 hours or 48 hours.

But as President, I cannot let the people's business be postponed over and over again. I've jotted down the numbers. There have been three dozen in the last decade – three dozen continuing resolutions – business as usual. And we can't have it. The President can only do this one thing: send that message back and say this is not a time for business as usual. The deficit is too important to the American people.

So, I expressed my appreciation to the Speaker, the majority leader in the Senate, the majority leader in the House, two Republican leaders – thanked them for coming together in a spirit of compromise to get an agreement that I strongly supported. It didn't have everything I wanted in there, but now I'm calling on those who did not vote for it on the Republican side and on the Democratic side to get up with the leadership and send down something that will take care of the people's business once and for all.

I am sorry that I have to do this, but I made very clear that I am not going to be a part of business as usual when we have one deficit after another piling up. Had enough of it, and I think the American people have had enough of it.

Q. What changed your mind, sir?

Q. Mr. Mitchell (House majority leader) came out here a minute ago and said that this served no useful purpose. What useful purpose?

The President. We have a disagreement with him. I think it disciplines the United States Congress, Democrats and Republicans. They're the ones that have to pass this budget, and they ought to get on with it. And the leaders, to their credit, tried. But a lot of Members think they can get a free shot, right and left. What this message says is: No more business as usual. So, we did have a difference on that particular point. I think both the Speaker and the majority leader did not want me to do this.

But look, let me take you guys back a while. In August I wanted to keep the Congress in. That story was written. And I've listened to the leadership, both Republicans and Democrats, said no we'll acquiesce – because they said that to keep the Congress here in August will be counterproductive: "Everybody will be angry with you. But the way to get it done is with the discipline of the calendar running after the summer recess."

And so, I acquiesced. I compromised. I gave. I'm not going to do it anymore. I'm very sorry if people are inconvenienced but I am not going to be a part of business as usual by the United States Congress.

Q. Mr. President, Senator Dole (Republican leader) said that you had agreed to send up a new short-term spending bill that would include spending cuts – a sequester. Could you tell us something about that?

The President. I'm going to stay out of exactly what we're going to do and let the leaders handle the details of this now. It's in the Congress, and I still strongly support the agreement that both Democrat leaders and Republican leaders came down on. And I'll say this: I do think that there's a lot of agreement and good will still existing for that. It's not going to be passed exactly that way. It was defeated. But let's leave the details of negotiation on that to the Congress – starting back in right now. They're going to have to contend with this veto I sent up – and obviously, I want to see that veto sustained.

Q. You say no more business as usual – in one breath you say no more CR's (continuing resolutions), and in the next breath Dole says there's some CR which is –

The President. Well, if it has some discipline – what I'm saying is, I want to see the system disciplined. If what Bob Dole said is correct – I'll sign one if it puts some discipline on the system. And if it doesn't discipline on the system, then I stay with my current position. No, excuse me, I'm glad you brought that up, because I would strongly support that.

Q. Mr. President, the leadership made a strong point in saying that it's the average Americans who are going to be hurt, the Federal workers and so forth. It's not Congressmen, but average Americans who are going to be strongly hurt by this.

The President. The average American is smart. The average American is smart. The average American knows what's going on,

I think. And I think they know that the Congress will continue to kick this can down the road and that they've got to act. I am very sorry for people that are inconvenienced by this or hurt by this. But this is the only device one has for making something happen, and that is to get the Congress to act, to do its business.

Q. Mr. President, you seem to be blaming Congress, but in fact, a lot of their constituents are the ones that urged them to vote against this. They say it's unfair – the burden is unfairly divided, that the poor and the middle class are paying too much. Is it possible that maybe this program that you proposed with the leaders just was not acceptable to the American public?

The President. Well, certain aspects of it might well not have been acceptable to the American public on both the right or the left. But when you're trying to do the country's business, I've discovered you have to compromise from time to time, and that's exactly what I did. Took a few shots in the process, but it doesn't matter. What matters is, let's move this process ahead now.

But, yes, you're right – some people didn't like one aspect or another. We had Republicans jumping up on our side of the aisle and saying, "I'll vote for it if you change this," or "I don't like this part of it, but if you change that – " And similarly, you've got people that you were quoting that were on the other side.

But at times, one has to come together to do the country's business for the overall good. And these outrageous deficits cannot be permitted to go on and on and on and on. I'm worried about international markets. I'm worried about this country – the opinion that it can't take care of its fiscal business.

And to their leaders' credit, Democrat and Republican, they tried very hard. They failed to get a majority on the Democratic side. And Republican leaders, with the help from the President and all I could bring to bear on it – we failed, because we had people – were looking at one narrow part of the package and not at the overall good. And I am hopeful now that with the urgency this veto brings to bear on the situation, that reasonable people, men and women in the Congress, can come together.

Q. Mr. President, what kind of progress is being made on a new budget resolution? And sources on the Hill are saying that there is growing support for raising the tax rates of the wealthy in exchange, perhaps, for the cuts on premiums for Medicare. But you have opposed that in the past. Are you willing to give on tax rates for the wealthy?

The President. I don't know the answer to your question. They're just going back up now to try. I like the parameters of the other deal wherein I compromise. We've got people – your question reflects the views on the more liberal or left side of the political spectrum – who raised those questions. We have some on the right side of the political spectrum coming at the process from another way.

Now, I say: Let them go up and negotiate it. This is the business of the Congress. And our people will stay in touch. I won't mislead them. If there's something that's so outrageous I can't accept it. I'll let them know at the beginning so they don't waste their time. But we're flexible. I've already compromised. And I'm not saying that I can't take a look at new proposals. But you've got to put together a majority in the Congress, and that's where the leaders are having great difficulty.

Q. Following up on that, members of your own party dislike the deal so much, how could you and your advisers have misjudged the sentiments of members of your own party?

The President. Because it's easy when you don't have to be responsible for something. It's easy to just get up and say, hey, I've got an election in 3 weeks, and I'm going to stand up against this particular package – Medicare, the taxes, the home heating oil, or the fact there's not enough growth or not enough incentive. Any individual Member can do that. Maybe it plays well at home. The President and the leadership of both Houses have to be responsible for the overall good of the country, have to make something happen. I can't get it done just my way. I don't control both Houses of Congress. I'd love to think that that luxury would come by way someday, but it hasn't. Therefore, we've had to compromise. So, I will keep trying in that spirit – that cooperative, positive spirit.

But when it comes to the discipline that comes from saying. "I'm sorry, no more business as usual," that's where I can stand up. I don't need a consultation to do that. I've got plenty of advice on one side of that question and the other. But I am absolutely convinced this is right.

Even those who are inconvenienced by this are going to say, thank God, we'll get the American people's business of getting this deficit under control done. That's my objective. I think every parent out there who sees his kid's future being mortgaged by the outrageous deficit, sees a shaky economy that's being affected by prolonging these deliberations, will be grateful in the long run. In the meantime, we've got to take a little heat.

Q. Mr. President, the budget resolution that failed is one that you worked hard for. Despite the fact that you gave a national televised speech, despite the fact that your popularity is very high – and you failed to sway even a majority of votes in your own party. Does that concern you, and do you think this is a major setback for your Presidency?

The President. No, I don't think that at all. But I do think – yes, it concerns me. I'd like everybody to do it exactly the way I want, but it doesn't work that way. So, now we have to have a little discipline –

Q. Mr. President –

The President. – nice guy stuff, and we'll try. *It's a tough decision; it's not an easy decision I've made, but it is the right decision. So, I'm disappointed they didn't do it my way. But I'm in here to do what is best for the country, and what is best for the country is to get this deficit under control, to get this economy moving again, and to see people at jobs, not out on some welfare line. And that's what's at stake here – economic soundness of the United States.*

We've got a lot of things going on in the world, and a strong economy is vital to what I want to see achieved in this country. So, you have to take some hits. I mean, you don't get it done exactly your own way.

But I read these speculative stories. Tomorrow, there's going to be another vote. Tomorrow, somebody else will move the previous question or second the motion, or some committee chairman will jump up and say, hey, what about me – my little empire is being invaded here. And I'll say, hey, the President's the guy that has to look at the overall picture.

I can understand Congressmen doing that. But we came together on a deal. We worked for it. Everybody had a chance to posture that didn't like it. They have no responsibility. But I feel a certain responsibility to the American people to move something forward here – want a compromise. Now we're going to say: We'll try it this way. No more business as usual. Do not just keep putting off the day of reckoning. And I don't want to be a part of that, and that's why I've had to veto this resolution.

Q. Mr. President, you've talked a lot about discipline today. Do you think the American people on average are willing to accept the discipline of a tough budget?

The President. That's a good question. And if you look at the vote in the House of Representatives, you might say no. But I think in the final analysis the answer will be yes, because I think we sometimes underestimate the intelligence of the American people. I can see where a Congressman can jump up on a specific spending program that'll help him in his district. I can see when somebody will give you the broad tax speech or help him in his district.

But in the final analysis, what the American people look at is: Do we have an economy in which I can feed my family, where I can have opportunity to work for a living, and where I can put a little aside to educate my kids? And therein lies the problem, because that's what we're working for – is we're trying to get this Federal deficit down.

But I think you raise a good point. I think a lot of these Congressmen can jump up without any responsibility for running the country, or even cooperating with their leaders, and make a point that's very happy for the home folks. But I think that view underestimates the overall intelligence of the American people, whether conservative, whether a guy's working on a factory line someplace, whether he's an investor someplace.

That's why I think this is very important that the Congress now finally come to grips with this.

Q. There's some talk about this special challenge to Civiletti.

Q. Mr. President, it sounds like you're now saying: Hands off. It's up to the congressional leaders to do the negotiating.

The President. They've already started up the road there to go to Congress and start negotiating. But, no, we've made very clear that we're continuing to help. I don't want to mislead them. There are certain things I can accept. There are certain things I can't. So, I think it's very important that our able team, in whom I have total confidence, stay in touch with them.

Q. But not sit at the negotiating table with them?

The President. Oh, I think they'll be there. I think it all depends on what forum. I think there is some feeling, Ann [Ann Devroy, Washington Post], that on the part of Members, both Democrat and Republicans – hey, you summiteers handed us a deal. Well, what the heck? I mean, how do you expect to get as far along toward an agreement as we did get? But what I want to do is facilitate it. And if they want to know where the White House is, fine. If they want the ideas that largely led to an agreement, fine, and I think they will. But we're not going to force our way in. This is the business of the Congress. The American people know that. They know that the President doesn't pass the budget and doesn't vote on all this stuff. It's the Congress who does it.

So, I'm not trying to assign blame. I'm simply saying, we're available. We want to talk- fine. I think both leaders have indicated they wanted to stay in fairly close touch with the White House.

Q. Mr. President, there is some talk of a constitutional challenge to Civiletti on the bill that the Attorney General's opinion is not sufficient to run the Government, and that violates section 7 of the Constitution.

The President. I haven't heard anything about that.

Q. Mr. President, are you going to cancel your campaign schedule next week if this impasse is not resolved?

The President. I don't know. I've got to cancel everything that has to do with government, I guess. Maybe that's a good chance to get out there in the political process.

Q. How long can you hold out? How long can you let the Government stay shut down before you decide to toss –

The President. Watch and learn.

Q. How long do you think the Government can stay shut before –

The President. It's not a question of how long I can take it; it's how long the Congress can take it. But Congress is where the action is. It's the Congress that has to pass this in the House and in the Senate. That's where the action is. They've postponed this tough decision as I've mentioned – how many – 30-some times. And we just can't have it. The American people are saying, "I want something done about this." That's where the focus will be.

So, I don't think it's a question of taking heat here or these guys marching out here about honking their horns on taxes. They know I don't like taxes. You get some other guy in Washington out here with a little placard, demonstrating – something about the government employees – we've been supporters of the government employees. But we cannot have business as usual.

The American people – I don't know about inside the beltway, but outside they are fed up with business as usual, and so am I. I wish I had total control so we could do it exactly my way, but we don't. So, I've compromised. Now we're prepared to say, I'm not going to accept a resolution that just postpones it. I've told you I tried that approach.

I tried it in August. Let everybody go home on vacation when I had some good, sound advice I probably should have taken: Make the Congress stay in August. And I listened to the leaders, and they said: "Oh, please don't do that. It will be counterproductive." Now they're saying to me: "Please don't veto this. It will be counterproductive." When do the American people have a say? They want to see this deficit under control. And I don't have many weapons here as President, but one is the veto. When I do it, cast it on principle, I hope it is supported.

Q. What's happened to the prestige –

Q. If Dole sends up another CR, if the Congress sends up a CR with sequestration, when could that happen? Do you have some timeframe?

The President. I don't know.

Q. Could it happen the next couple of days, sir?

The President. Oh, yes, absolutely. It could happen this afternoon.

Q. It could happen this afternoon?

The President. Sure. Whether we – together? I'm not that certain. Perhaps it's a little oversimplification because they're telling me there are some difficult problems right and left, both sides. But, no, they're going right back to negotiating. Let's hope it does. That's the way to serve the constituents.

If it came up this afternoon, sir, would you sign it this afternoon?

The President. It depends what it is. I'll be around.

Q. You have vetoed the CR?

The President. Yes – well, I haven't actually signed it, but I've got to rush right in there now and do that and send it up to the Hill. They know that they've-

Last question.

Q. Why did you change your mind?

Q. What's all this done to the prestige and influence of you and your office?

The President. Well, I think it will demonstrate that there is some power in the Presidency to compel the Congress to do something, and I think that's good.

Q. You are vetoing, though?

The President. Oh, yes. It hasn't been vetoed yet, but I need a typewriter in there to get it done. By the time we finish this press conference that has gone longer than I thought, it'll – probably be typed up.

Q. Might you trade the bubble for capital gains now? Do you foresee that as a compromise?

The President. The negotiators in the Congress have a lot of flexibility. I remain in a flexible frame of mind. Certain things I can accept and can't. But I'd like to think that now those who postured on one side or another with no responsibility will join the leaders, Republican and Democrat, and say: Hey, we've got a responsibility to the overall good here. We can no longer just give a speech. We've got to pitch in and come together. And that's what my pitch is.

And that's why I'm doing it and doing this veto – saying, hey, no more business as usual. And I think people understand that sometimes a President has to make a difficult decision. So, I don't worry about the prestige. I was elected to do what – in a case like this – what I think is best and in the national interest. And that's exactly what I'm doing.

Thank you all very much.

Q. Are you going to type those up yourself?

The President. Yes, but I didn't give you the full load.

Note: The President's 62d news conference began at 11:30 a.m. on the West Driveway of the White House. A tape was not available for verification of the content of this new conference.

Remarks on the Federal Budget Agreement and an Exchange With Reporters in Honolulu, Hawaii. October 27, 1990

The President. Let me start with a statement, and then be glad to take some questions. But I've just been informed that the United States Senate has just passed the House-Senate conference report on the budget. This completes congressional action on an agreement to reduce the Federal deficit by over $490 billion over the next 5 years.

This budget blueprint represents corrective action on a pattern of Federal spending gone out of control. We have put on the brakes, and the process has sometimes been painful. But I will sign this legislation because, for the first time, it makes significant and long-term cuts in Federal spending that should have a positive impact on America's economic future. *All political points of view have sacrificed to bring this agreement about. And, needless to say, I don't like raising taxes and never will, but there is a price to divided government, and that means that I have had to compromise on items that I feel strongly about in order to do what I think is best for the country, and that is to reach an agreement.*

At the same time, we've cut Federal spending programs and applied some self-discipline, steps that also may not be popular. But the essential ingredient which has produced bipartisan agreement is that we must get the deficit down, get interest rates down, and keep America moving. And I might add, I'm told that the final enforcement provisions are very, very strong, so that we're guarding against more spending – out-of-control spending next year and into the future, covered by this agreement.

In addition, I am pleased that many of my proposals on child care are incorporated in this budget reconciliation bill. The legislation provides tax credits, grants, and vouchers that put choice in the hands of parents rather than in the hands of bureaucrats. So, I'm very pleased about the childcare provision, something I've been fighting for.

I intend to sign the agreement. And I will also review closely the various appropriations bills to make sure that they conform to this new spending agreement. We've made the tough decisions, and now it's time to move on.

And I am pleased that the Congress also has passed historic Clean Air Act amendments which will reduce acid rain, urban smog, and toxic air pollutions. We proposed this far-reaching environmental cleanup legislation some 15 months ago with the hope that this initiative by the administration would break the logjam that had prevented a clean air bill from being passed previously. This is an important milestone in preserving and protecting America's natural resources, and I look forward to signing the bill.

I want to conclude by thanking everyone involved, including the bipartisan leadership in Congress for their tireless efforts in forging and passing the new budget agreement. The Speaker (Thomas S. Foley), Minority Leader Bob Michel, the Majority Leader Dick Gephardt, Senator Mitchell, and Senator Dole have all had to compromise some. And they've stayed with it long, long hours, trying to hammer out this agreement, so I want to take this opportunity to thank them.

I'll be glad to take a few questions, and then we've got to head on.

Budget Agreement

Q. Mr. President, you signed on to this budget agreement and your negotiators negotiated it with Congress, including the tax increases that you vowed you wouldn't do when you ran for office. Are you prepared now to give it a sound endorsement and urge Republican candidates to go out and sell it to the voters as well –

The President. No –

Q. – or are you going to turn your back on it and blame the Democrats for the tax increases that you agreed with?

The President. I'm going to say, look, I've reluctantly signed this. There are things in it that if I controlled both Houses of Congress, wouldn't be in it, and I think the Democrats will be saying the same thing. I noticed some of them saying yesterday that they felt we ought to have higher income tax rates. One of the things I'm glad about is that we've held the line on income tax rates.

A handful of the wealthiest went up, and 10 times that many of the upper middle income came down. Some went from 28 to 31; others came down from 33 to 31. There are certain things in it that I can strongly advocate. There are some things in it that I had to gag and digest. And so, that's the approach I'm going to be taking, and expect everyone else will too.

Q. Mr. President, you said it's time to move on. Do you have any fear or do you think – expectation that the whole fiasco over the last couple of weeks is going to haunt you in the election?

The President. No, I don't think so at all. Sometimes the President has to make a tough call; this is one of them I'll be right out on the campaign trail advocating the election of more Republicans to the Congress. And we wouldn't have been in this mess if we had that.

Q. Mr. President, how can you go out now and blame Democrats, criticize Democrats, when in fact they, more than Republicans, helped you get this budget package – which you supported – passed?

The President. Hey, listen, that shows that I don't like everything in the package. I mean, if I were all that enthusiastic about it you'd have seen more Republicans voting for it. So, nobody got it exactly the way he or she wanted, but now it's behind us. As soon as I sign it, that's behind us. And I hope it will have the effect of bringing interest rates down. But the philosophy of holding the line on spending and holding the line on taxes is my philosophy. And I will be clearly advocating that.

Taxes

Q. What message will you use now, then, to replace your "no new taxes" pledge? Everybody is very accustomed to that, all the Republicans. And I just want to know what slogan or –

The President. Let me be clear: I'm not in favor of new taxes. I'll repeat that over and over and over again. And this one compromise where we begrudgingly had to accept revenue increases is the exception that proves the rule. That's the way I'll handle it.

Q. The exception that proves what rule?

The President. The rule that I'm strongly opposed to raising taxes on the American people and that we ought to do a better job of controlling spending. And I think we can. So, that's the message, loud and clear.

Q. Will you reinstate today your "no new taxes" pledge, perhaps "no new taxes"? Do you think – remember after '86 that the congress passed a resolution saying they wouldn't tamper with it for 5 years. Do you think now the line should be drawn again and, having made this compromise, you should now hold the line on taxes again?

The President. Absolutely going to hold the line on taxes. And hopefully – the big thing is to hold the line on spending so nobody will come up and try to propose new taxes.

But I noticed one of the Democratic leaders said yesterday, well, he wants to raise income tax rates. And he's going to have a whale of a fight on it. This was a one-time compromise.

Budget Agreement

Q. You really don't seem very enthusiastic about this budget deal. You don't seem euphoric after all you and the others have been through –

The President. That's right. You got it.

Q. – and I might note that it doesn't appear to meet your own objectives. You've been insisting on a $500-billion deficit reduction target – now only $490 billion. Plus I understand the deal is based on rosy economic assumptions over which there is much disagreement. How do you feel?

The President. I feel that it's been a long arduous battle. And I feel that every once in a while the President has to do something he doesn't like, and that is to compromise. And I did that here. So,

I'm glad it's over, and I have to say that the hours that the Democratic leaders and the Republican leaders spent working this problem has just been exhausting for everybody, including me, although they did much more of the work. So, I'm glad it's behind us, and I feel good that it's behind us, but I can't be euphoric about every provision in this bill.

I am very encouraged about the enforcement provisions because they are strong. And no guy can go out and put in a new program without the offset. The guarantees of enforcement are strong, and I'm going to do my level best to see that they stay strong.

So, you're trying to describe mood. I am pleased it's behind us, and I will be out vigorously campaigning on the campaign trail for more Republicans who feel as I do about holding the line on taxes and about spending. And we have a difference of opinion. You have more people that wanted to increase, on the Democratic side, these permissive spending programs. So, the philosophy, the fundamental philosophical underpinning – yes, I haven't changed my view on that, and I'm sure the liberal Democrats haven't either. But we'll take that case to the American people.

Q. Can you really show the American people with all your heart that this is a good deal?

The President. Parts of it are good. No, I can't say this is the best thing that's happened to us since sliced bread or the elimination of broccoli. It has got some good things in it, but if we re doing it my way, or the Republican leader in the Senate's way, or the Republican leader in the House's way, it would be very, very different.

But I think it is good that we have a $490 billion – I'd like to have seen $500 billion, but this is a lot of money – $490 billion, enforceable deficit reduction program. And the part, the overall part, I am enthusiastic about. But how we got it – I reserve the right to be as critical as the next person on that.

Republican Campaign Strategy

Q. Mr. President, do you think it was proper for the Republican Congressional Campaign Committee to recommend that the party's candidate's distance themselves from the President on this?

The President. No, I want everybody to be right with me on everything I do.

Q. Is the architect of that strategy, Ed Rollins (cochairman of the committee), history as far as you're concerned?

The President. That is inside the belt-way — I know how people love that. They thrive on it. I don't . And you know, ever since I got out around the country, not one person has sidled up to me and asked me about that particular incident. And I'm going to keep my sights set on the big picture and not accommodate you when you want me to go back into that. I understand it; I understand it because people thrive — what was that, Lori [Lori Santos, United Press International]?

Q. Does he know?

Q. Is he out?

Q. Is he out?

The President. I'm not discussing it because it would divert me from the major goal, which is to elect more Republicans to agree, as I do — hold the line on taxes and spending, get people back to work in this country by getting interest rates down, and empowering people, not programs and bureaucrats. So, I get diverted if you try to get me into some little staff matter.

Representative Gingrich

Q. Conspicuously missing from that list of leaders that you recited, Mr. President, was the name of Newt Gingrich. Some people have suggested that you could have gotten a better deal if he had not led the Republican revolt a couple of weeks ago. Do you think that he should remain in his leadership position because of his actions?

The President. Remember – what was the give-and-take in the debate when Ronald Reagan said, there you go again trying to get me caught up in something divisive. Newt Gingrich stood out there in the White House – I'm not sure you were there that day – and strongly endorsed Republican unity, and that's exactly what should happen. So, please don't ask me to relive the agony of a budget agreement that I am glad is signed and is now behind us.

Mr. Fitzwater. One final question.

Budget Agreement

Q. Do you feel that the Republican Party has been badly hurt by this –

The President. No.

Q. – and aren't you sorry that you couldn't have gotten more Republican votes?

The President. I'm not particularly sorry because a lot of the Members feel as I do: They were gagging on certain provisions, but glad that it's passed. And I think if this compromise had been perfect from the Republican side, you'd have seen – obviously have many, many more votes. So, I think those that didn't vote against it, on both sides, had problems with it. Some on the Democratic side were saying, we want to raise income tax rates on the American people more. That's literally what they wanted to do. They called it soak the rich, but what they meant was — when that bill that they passed in the Congress, with that indexing — went after every working man and woman in this country. And that's the old tax-and-spend view, and some of them didn't feel it went far enough. Some on our side didn't like anything to do with revenues; that's more along my line of thinking.

So, I think that's history now, but I have no rancor about it. I'm just glad it's passed. I wish it had been passed when we had the summit agreement, and we'd have been much further along.

But I don't — back to the first part of your question- no, I sense strong enthusiasm for Republican candidates., And I think we've been caught up in a bit of an inside smoke screen here. But let's see now how we do. I'm going to be out there, working my heart out for Republican candidates who feel as I do that we ought to hold the line on taxes and that we ought to curtail spending.

Q. Are we headed for another recession?

The President. The economy is sluggish, and there's no question about that. And I am convinced, whether I like every paragraph of this or not, that this is good medicine for the economy, particularly if the Federal Reserve Board now follows up with lowering interest rates. You know, that is what's needed, and I'm not here to do anything other than to state that principle. But I listened carefully to [Federal Reserve Board Chairman] Alan Greenspan's testimony, and I was encouraged that interest rates might come down. Better than any program is getting these rates down so economic growth gets stimulated.

Persian Gulf Crisis

Q. Just to switch to the Gulf crisis for a moment. Secretary

Cheney indicates we may send as many as 100,000 new troops in and a lot more tanks. What's the purpose, sir, if it's not to take offensive action and get engaged in combat with Iraq?

The President. Just a minute. Power outage here.

We have not announced what we are going to do in terms of additional troops. We have been still, as everybody around the world knows, still moving forces. The purpose is to make clear to Saddam Hussein [President of Iraq] that his aggression will not stand. What I do in the future will be determined after I have a discussion with Dick Cheney and the Chairman of the Joint Chiefs [Colin L. Powell], and Secretary Baker, which I expect we'll be doing – looking for help with Brent – when we get back. Maybe we'll have more to say about that then.

But I believe a couple of things on this. One, I think Saddam Hussein really felt that nobody was going to move against his aggression in Kuwait. I also believe that he really intended to threaten Saudi Arabia – or else why did he move all his armor south to the Saudi border? I think as he sees the U.S. forces moving in conjunction with many Arab country forces, in conjunction with many European country forces on land on the sea, that he's taking another look. Because we are deadly serious. I want to see these economic sanctions work.

I'm not too good at the emotional side of it, but when you talk to the parents and spouses of our kids halfway around the world, it makes a real impact on you. I remember when I got off the plane at the Marine base, and they were saying, "Take care of my husband," and yet, "We back you 100 percent." So, I don't think that's a conflict exactly, but I want to take care of every young man and woman that's serving the United States halfway around the world. But they want, and I want, to see that Saddam's aggression is unrewarded and, indeed, repudiated. So, the moving of U.S. force up to now has sent a strong signal to him. We have the finest, most highly motivated, best trained, best equipped Armed Forces in the world. And they're right there. They're right there in substantial numbers – land, air, and sea.

Now, Mr. Saddam Hussein, get out of Kuwait with no condition. This talk of some condition – that is unacceptable not just to the United States but to the other countries around the world. I just got off the phone talking to President Mubarak [of Egypt] – steadfast friend to the United States. He's made that same message loud and clear. On his travels he's heard it from those who were side by side with us in the Gulf, and then he's told his visitors that. So, we're staying pretty well together on this end.

Just a couple of more, and then I really have to get going. One, two, three over here, and then I'm – you're history, Jessica – I've got to go.

Q. When you say you think that Saddam Hussein has gotten the message that we are deadly serious, do you think now that chances are better for a negotiated settlement of this situation than they were?

The President. I don't know about a negotiated settlement. There's nothing to negotiate, other than the acceptance of the United Nations-mandated resolutions. So, there's noting to negotiate. But in terms of a peaceful solution, I'm told that the economic effect are taking hold – effects of the sanctions – and that is encouraging. I'm told that he now sees that he's up against a substantial force that clearly could prevail in any battle. So, I'm hopeful that there will be a peaceful solution to this question. But there can be no preconditions. There can be no rewarding of aggression.

Q. There are two points to my question. There are some people who are saying that the U.S. continues to send in even more troops because the U.S. has underestimated the Iraqi troop strength. That, coupled with yesterday – apparently in Spain, President Gorbachev apparently said he notes a softening on the position of Saddam Hussein. Do you have any reason to believe there has been a softening? Has Mr. Gorbachev told you something you'd like to share with us? Has that softening manifested itself in any way?

The President. I have not noticed a softening, but I've heard more kind of little threads of talk of "negotiation" – that's all. Maybe that's what President Gorbachev is talking about. But he has not shared with me any feeling of a softening of public opinion. But what was the first part?

Q. Has the U.S. underestimated, perhaps, the troop strength of the Iraqis? Is that why we're continuing to send in more troops?

The President. No. I think it's true that Saddam Hussein beefed up his armor and his forces in Kuwait. From the original deployment, he then has stepped that up by pouring more armor in.

I'll never forget the day when he said, well, we're taking our people out of Kuwait, and they had one forlorn-looking soldier in the back of a truck waving goodbye – truck heading north – and then he had all his armor moving south. So, it was a sheer fraud. And he moved a heck of a lot of armor down against the Saudis. So, I'd leave it there, but I think that when you see a lot of force there, why, the free world and those of us that are allied together are going to say: Wait a minute! We're going to do what we've got to do to protect American life or Egyptian life or, in this instance, Syrian life or Saudi life. And that's why you're seeing a substantial movement of U.S. force and forces of other countries.

I keep repeating this because it's a very important point. It is not the United States versus Saddam Hussein; it is the United States, big majorities in the Arab world, and the United Nations versus Suddam Hussein. And that point – I keep making it because he is still trying to divide and weaken this strong coalition. And he's failing, he is failing miserably because all these countries are united against his brutal aggression.

Yes, Rita [Rita Beamish, Associated Press], and then Jessica. I'm recanting because I wasn't very kind. Go ahead.

Budget Agreement

Q. Just back on the budget for a minute. What do you think it says about your leadership and your ability to lead the party that you couldn't get more Republicans to stay with you and vote with you on this very important issue of the budget?

The President. I learned a lot from Ronald Reagan, with whom I worked closely and watched and learned. And in 19 – what was it – 82, when we had that big tax bill, I think we got fewer votes than we did today, and he went right out and did beautifully what he felt in his heart he should do, and say, look, I'm against increasing taxes and the American people know this. And he went right on about his business. And that agreement brought interest rates down. And we all went forth and said, wait a minute, every once in a while when you don't control Congress you don't get to do it exactly your way.

And so, I understand Republicans defecting from a package that they don't like. But a President, to make something happen, once in a great while has to make a significant compromise. And that's what I did. And I think the American people understand that. They know that I'm trying pretty hard, and they know that I have their interest at stake when I want to see interest rates down and more jobs for the working men and women in this country. And that's the way I'd handle that one.

Now, last one, Jessica, and then I am leaving.

Q. Irritable? Why would you be irritable?

The President. Thing aren't going exactly the way I want them done. I wish we could have got this deficit down without touching revenue. I wish that we could have got it done without all this inside-the-beltway furor because it's diverted me from major objectives.

Q. Do you feel – by Republicans in all of this –

The President. No, no, no. I feel happy about Republicans. I'm glad this is behind us, and I wish we had more of them. No matter what little philosophical wing of the party they're from, all of them would be better than what I face when I try to get stuff done from the Democrats. I mean, that's what it's all about.

Thank you all.

Q. Can you – no new taxes – read your lips again? [Laughter]

The President. Thank you so much. Read my what? [Laughter]

Q. Yes, that's right. We can't figure out which part of your anatomy.

Note: The President spoke at 12:15 p.m. at the Center for Cultural Interchange Between East and West. Marlin Fitzwater was Press Secretary to the President, and John H. Sununu was Chief of Staff to the President.

Remarks by the President
In State of the Union Address
January 28, 1992

THE PRESIDENT: Mr. Speaker and Mr. President, distinguished members of Congress, honored guests and fellow citizens. Thank you very much for that warm reception. You know, with the big buildup this address has had, I want to make sure it would be a big hit, but I couldn't convince Barbara to deliver it for me. (Applause.)

I see the Speaker and the Vice President are laughing. They saw what I did in Japan and they're just happy they're sitting behind me. (Laughter.)

I mean to speak tonight of big things, of big changes and the promises they hold, and of some big problems – and how, together, we can solve them and move our country forward as the undisputed leader of the age. (Applause.)

We gather tonight at a dramatic and deeply promising time in our history, and in the history of man on Earth. For in the past twelve months the world has known changes of almost biblical proportions. And even now, months after the failed coup that doomed a failed system, I'm not sure we've absorbed the full impact, the full import of what happened. But communism died this year. (Applause.)

Even as President, with the most fascinating possible vantage point, there were times when I was so busy managing progress and helping to lead change that I didn't always show the joy that was in my heart. But the biggest thing that has happened in the world in my life, in our lives, is this: By the grace of God, America won the Cold War. (Applause.)

I mean to speak this evening of the changes that can take place in our country now that we can stop making the sacrifices we had to make when we had an avowed enemy that was a superpower. Now we can look homeward even more, and move to set right what needs to be set right.

I will speak of those things. But let me tell you something I've been thinking these past few months. It's a kind of roll call of honor. For the Cold War didn't "end" – it was won. And I think of those who won it, in places like Korea, and Vietnam. And some of them didn't come back. Back then they were heroes, but this year they were victors. (Applause)

The long roll call – all the G.I. Joes and Janes, all the ones who fought faithfully for freedom, who hit the ground and sucked the dust and knew their share of horror. This may seem frivolous – and I don't mean it so – but it's moving to me how the world saw them.

The world saw not only their special valor, but their special style – their rambunctious, optimistic bravery, their do-or-die unity unhampered by class or race or region. What a group we've put forth, for generations now, from the ones who wrote "Kilroy was Here" on the walls of the German stalags, to those who left signs in the Iraqi desert that said, "I Saw Elvis." What a group of kids we've sent into the world. (Applause.)

And there's another to be singled out, though it may seem inelegant. I mean a mass of people called The American Taxpayer. No one ever thinks to thank the people who pay a country's bill, or an Alliance's bill. But for half a century now, the American people have shouldered the burden and paid taxes that were higher than they would have been to support a defense that was bigger than it would have been if imperial communism had never existed.

But it did – doesn't anymore. (Applause.)

And here's a fact I wouldn't mind the world acknowledging: The American taxpayer bore the brunt of the burden, and deserves a hunk of the glory. (Applause.)

And so now, for the first time in 35 years, our strategic bombers stand down. No longer are they on 'round-the-clock' alert. Tomorrow our children will go to school and study history and how plants grow. And they won't have, as my children did, air raid drills in which they crawl under their desks and cover their heads in case of nuclear war. My grandchildren don't have to do that, and won't have the bad dreams children had once, in decades past. There are still threats. But the long, drawn out dread is over. (Applause.)

A year ago tonight I spoke to you at a moment of high peril. American forces had just unleashed Operation Desert Storm. And after 40 days in the desert skies and four days on the ground, the men and women of America's Armed Forces, and our allies, accomplished the goals that I declared and that you endorsed: We liberated Kuwait. (Applause.)

Soon after, the Arab world and Israel sat down to talk seriously, and comprehensively, about peace – an historic first. And soon after that, at Christmas, the last American hostages came home. Our policies were vindicated. (Applause.)

Much good can come from the prudent use of power. And much good can come of this: A world once divided into two armed camps now recognizes one sole and pre-eminent power: the United States of America. (Applause.) And they regard this with no dread. For the world trusts us with power and the world is right. They trust us to be fair and restrained; they trust us to be on the side of decency; they trust us to do what's right.

I use those words advisedly. A few days after the war began, I received a telegram from Joanne Speicher, the wife of the first pilot killed in the Gulf, Lt. Commander Scott Speicher. Even in her grief she wanted me to know that some day, when her children were old enough, she would tell them "that their father went away to war because it was the right thing to do." She said it all. It was the right thing to do.

And we did it together. There were honest differences right here in this Chamber. But when the war began, you put partisanship aside and we supported our troops. This is still a time for pride, but this is no time to boast. For problems face us, and we must stand together once again and solve them, and not let our country down. (Applause.)

Two years ago I began planning cuts in military spending that reflected the changes of the new era. But now, this year, with imperial communism gone, that process can be accelerated. Tonight can tell you of dramatic changes in our strategic nuclear force. These are actions we are taking on our own because they are the right thing to do.

After completing 20 planes for which we have begun procurement, we will shut down further production of the B-2 bomber. (Applause.) We will cancel the small ICBM program. We will cease production of new warheads for our sea-based ballistic missiles. We will stop all new production of the Peacekeeper missile. And we will not purchase any more advanced cruise missiles.

This weekend I will meet at Camp David with Boris Yeltsin of the Russian Federation. I've informed President Yeltsin that if the Commonwealth, the former Soviet Union, will eliminate all land-based multiple warhead ballistic missiles, I will do the following: We will eliminate all Peacekeeper missiles. We will reduce the number of warheads on Minuteman missiles to one, and reduce the number of warheads on our sea-based missiles by about one-third. And we will convert a substantial portion of our strategic bombers to primarily conventional use.

President Yeltsin's early response has been very positive, and I expect our talks at Camp David to be fruitful.

I want you to know that for half a century, American presidents have longed to make such decisions and say such words. But even in the midst of celebration, we must keep caution as a friend. For the world is still a dangerous place. Only the dead have seen the end of conflict. And though yesterday's challenges are behind us, tomorrow's are being born.

The Secretary of Defense recommended these cuts after consultation with the Joint Chiefs of Staff. And I make them with confidence. But do not misunderstand me: The reductions I have approved will save us an additional $50 billion over the next five years. By 1997, we will have cut defense by 30 percent since I took office. These cuts are deep, and you must know my resolve: This deep, and no deeper. (Applause.)

To do less would be insensible to progress, but to do more would be ignorant of history. We must not go back to the days of "the hollow army". We cannot repeat the mistakes made twice in this century, when armistice was followed by recklessness, and defense was purged as if the world were permanently safe.

I remind you this evening that I have asked for your support in funding a program to protect our country from limited nuclear missile attack. We must have this protection because too many people in too many countries have access to nuclear arms. (Applause.) And I urge you again to pass the Strategic Defense Initiative – S.D.I. (Applause.)

There are those who say that now we can turn away from the world, that we have no special role, no special place. But we are the United States of America, the leader of the West that has become the leader of the world. And as long as I am President I will continue to lead in support of freedom everywhere – not out of arrogance, not out of altruism, but for the safety and security of our children. (Applause.)

This is a fact: Strength in the pursuit of peace is no vice; isolationism in the pursuit of security is no virtue. (Applause.)

And now to our troubles at home. They're not all economic; the primary problem is our economy. There are some good signs: Inflation, that thief, is down; and interest rates are down. But unemployment is too high, some industries are in trouble, and growth is not what it should be. Let me tell you right from the start and right from the heart: I know we're in hard times, but I know something else: This will not stand. (Applause.)

In this Chamber – in this Chamber, we can bring the same courage and sense of common purpose to the economy that we brought to Desert Storm. And we can defeat hard times together.

I believe you'll help. One reason is that you're patriots and you want the best for your country. And I believe that in your hearts you want to put partisanship aside and get the job done because it's the right thing to do.

The power of America rests in a stirring but simple idea: That people will do great things if only you set them free. Well, we're going to set the economy free, for if this age of miracles and wonders has taught us anything, it's that if we can change the world, we can change America.

We must encourage investment. We must make it easier for people to invest money and create new products, new industries, and new jobs. We must clear away the obstacles to growth – high taxes, high regulation, red tape, and, yes, wasteful government spending. (Applause.)

None of this will happen with a snap of the fingers, but it will happen. And the test of a plan isn't whether it's called new or dazzling. The American people aren't impressed by gimmicks; they're smarter on this score than all of us in this room. The only test of a plan is, is it sound and will it work?

We must have a short-term plan to address our immediate needs and heat up the economy. And then we need a longer-term plan to keep combustion going and to guarantee our place in the world economy.

There are certain things that a President can do without Congress, and I'm going to do them. I have, this evening, asked major Cabinet departments and federal agencies to institute a 90-day moratorium on any new federal regulations that could hinder growth. (Applause.) In those 90 days major departments and agencies will carry out a top-to-bottom review of all regulations, old and new – to stop the ones that will hurt growth, and speed up those that will help growth.

Further, for the untold number of hard-working, responsible American workers and businessmen and women who've been forced to go without needed bank loans, the banking credit crunch must end. (Applause.) I won't neglect my responsibility for sound regulations that serve the public good, but regulatory overkill must be stopped. (Applause.) And I've instructed our government regulators to stop it. (Applause.)

I have directed Cabinet departments and federal agencies, to speed up progrowth expenditures as quickly as possible. This should put an extra $10 billion into the economy in the next six months. And our new transportation bill provides more than $150 billion for construction and maintenance projects that are vital to our growth and well-being. And that means jobs building roads, jobs building bridges, and jobs building railways.

And I have, this evening, directed the Secretary of the Treasury to change the federal tax withholding tables. With this change, millions of Americans, from whom the government withholds more than necessary, can now choose to have the government withhold less from their paychecks. Something tells me a number of taxpayers may take us up on this. This initiative could return about $25 billion back into our economy over the next 12 months – money people can use to help pay for clothing, college, or to get a new car. Finally, working with the Federal Reserve, we will continue to support monetary policy that keeps both interest rates and inflation down.

Now, these are the things I can do. And now, members of Congress, let me tell you what you can do for your country. (Applause.) You must pass the other elements of my plan to meet our economic needs. Everyone knows that investment spurs recovery. I am proposing this evening a change in the alternative minimum tax, and the creation of a new 15-percent investment tax allowance. (Applause.) This will encourage businesses to accelerate investment and bring people back to work.

Real estate has led our economy out of almost all the tough times we've ever had. Once building starts, carpenters and plumbers work, people buy homes and take out mortgages. My plan would modify the passive loss rule for active real estate developers. (Applause.) And it would make it easier for pension plans to purchase real estate.

For those Americans who dream of buying a first home, but who can't quite afford it, my plan would allow first-time homebuyers to withdraw savings from IRAs without penalty and provide a $5,000 tax credit for the first purchase of that home. (Applause.)

And finally, my immediate plan calls on Congress to give crucial help to people who own a home, to everyone who has a business, or a farm, or a single investment.

This time, at this hour, I cannot take no for an answer: You must cut the capital gains tax on the people of our country. (Applause.) Never has an issue been more demagogued by its opponents. (Applause.) But the demagogues are wrong – they are wrong and they know it. Sixty percent of the people who benefit from lower capital gains have incomes under $50,000. A cut in the capital gains tax increases jobs and helps just about everyone in our country. (Applause.) And so I'm asking you to cut the capital gains tax to a maximum of 15.4 percent. (Applause.)

And I'll tell you, those of you who say, oh, no, someone who's comfortable may benefit from that, you kind of remind me of the old definition of the Puritan who couldn't sleep at night, worrying that somehow someone somewhere was out having a good time. (Applause.)

The opponents of this measure – and those who have authored various so-called soak-the-rich bills that are floating around this Chamber – should be reminded of something: When they aim at the big guy they usually hit the little guy. And maybe it's time that stopped. (Applause.)

This, then, is my short-term plan. Your part, members of Congress, requires enactment of these common-sense proposals that will have a strong effect on the economy – without breaking the budget agreement and without raising tax rates. (Applause.)

While my plan is being passed and kicking in, we've go to care for those in trouble today. I have provided for up to $4.4 billion in my budget to extend federal unemployment benefits. And I ask for congressional action right away. (Applause.) And I thank the committee. (Applause.) Well, at last.

And let's be frank. Let's be frank. Let me level with you. I know and you know that my plan is unveiled in a political season. (Laughter.) I know and you know that everything I propose will be viewed by some in merely partisan terms. But I ask you to know what is in my heart, and aim is to increase our nation's good. I'm doing what I think is right; I am proposing what I know will help. (Applause.)

I pride myself that I'm a prudent man and I believe that patience is a virtue. But *I understand that politics is, for some, a game – and that sometimes the game is to stop all progress and then decry the lack of improvement. (Laughter.) But let me tell you: far more important than my political future – and far more important than yours – is the well-being of our country. (Applause.) Members of this Chamber are practical people, and I know you won't resent some practical advice. When people put their party's fortunes – whatever the party, whatever side of this aisle – before the public good, they court defeat not only for their country, but for themselves.* And they will certainly deserve it. (Applause.)

I submit my plan tomorrow, and I'm asking you to pass it by March 20th. (Applause.) And I ask the American people to let you know they want this action by March 20th.

From the day after that, if it must be, the battle is joined. And you know, when principle is at stake I relish a good fair fight. (Applause.)

I said my plan has two parts, and it does. And it's the second part that is the heart of the matter. For it's not enough to get an immediate burst, we need long-term improvement in our economic position.

We all know that the key to our economic future is to ensure that America continues an economic leader of the world. We have that in our power. Here, then, is my long-term plan to guarantee our future.

First, trade: We will work to break down the walls that stop world trade. We will work to open markets everywhere. And in our major trade negotiations I will continue pushing to eliminate tariffs and subsidies that damage America's farmers and workers. (Applause.)

And we'll get more good American jobs within our own hemisphere through the North American Free Trade Agreement, and through the Enterprise for the Americas Initiative. But changes are here, and more are coming. The workplace of the future will demand more highly-skilled workers than ever – more people who are computer-literate, highly-educated. We must be the world's leader in education. And we must revolutionize America's schools. (Applause.)

My America 2000 strategy will help us reach that goal. My plan will give parents more choice, give teachers more flexibility, and help communities create New American Schools. (Applause.) Thirty states across the nation have established America 2000 programs. Hundreds of cities and towns have joined in. Now Congress must join this great movement: Pass my proposals for New American schools.

That was my second long-term proposal, and here's my third: We must make common-sense investments that will help us compete, long-term in the marketplace. We must encourage research and development. My plan is to make the R&D tax credit permanent, and to provide record levels of support – (applause) – over $76 billion this year alone – for people who will explore the promise of emerging technologies. (Applause.)

Fourth, we must do something about crime and drugs. (Applause.) It is time for a major, renewed investment in fighting violent street crime. It saps our strength and hurts our faith in our society, and in our future together. Surely, a tired woman on her way to work at 6:00 a.m. in the morning on a subway deserves the right to get there safely. (Applause.) And surely it's true that everyone who changes his or her life because of crime, from those afraid to go out at night to those afraid to walk in the parks they pay for, surely these people have been denied a basic civil right. (Applause.)

It is time to restore it. Congress, pass my comprehensive crime bill. (Applause.) It is tough on criminals and supportive of police, and it has been languishing in these hollowed halls for years now. Pass it. Help your country. (Applause.)

And fifth, I ask you tonight to fund our HOPE housing proposal and to pass my enterprise zone legislation, which will get businesses into the inner city. We must empower the poor with the pride that comes from owning a home, getting a job, becoming a part of things. (Applause.) My plan would encourage real estate construction by extending tax incentives for mortgage revenue bonds and low income housing. (Applause.)

And I ask tonight for record expenditures for the program that helps children born into want move into excellence, Head Start. (Applause.)

Step six – we must reform our health care system. (Applause.) For this, too, bears on whether or not we can compete in the world. American health costs have been exploding. This year America will spend over $800 billion on health, and that is expected to grow to $1.6 trillion by the end of the decade. We simply cannot afford this.

The cost of health care shows up not only in your family budget, but in the price of everything we buy and everything we sell. When health coverage for a fellow on an assembly line costs thousands of dollars, the cost goes into the products he makes and you pay the bill.

We must make a choice. Now, some pretend we can have it both ways. They call it "play or pay", but that expensive approach is unstable. It will mean higher taxes, fewer jobs and, eventually, a system under complete government control.

Really, there are only two options. And we can move toward a nationalized system – (applause) – a system which will restrict patient choice in picking a doctor and force the government to ration services arbitrarily. And what we'll get is patients in long lines, indifferent service, and a huge new tax burden. (Applause.) Or we can reform our own private health care system, which still gives us, for all its flaws, the best quality health care in the world. (Applause.)

Well, let's build on our strengths. My plan provides insurance security for all Americans, while preserving and increasing the idea of choice. We make basic health insurance affordable for all low-income people not now covered, and we do it by providing a health insurance tax credit of up to $3,750 for each low-income family. And the middle class gets help, too. And by reforming the health insurance market, my plan assures that Americans will have access to basic health insurance even if they change jobs or develop serious health problems.

We must bring costs under control, preserve quality, preserve choice and reduce the people's nagging daily worry about health insurance. My plan, the details of which I will announce very shortly, does just that.

And seventh, we must get the federal deficit under control. (Applause.) We now have in law enforceable spending caps and a requirement that we pay for the programs we create. There are those in congress who would ease that discipline now, but I cannot let them do it, and I won't. (Applause.)

My plan would freeze all domestic discretionary budget authority, which means no more next year than this year. (Applause.) I will not tamper with Social Security – (applause) – but I would put real caps on the growth of uncontrolled spending. And I would also freeze federal domestic government employment. (Applause.)

And with the help of Congress, my plan will get rid of 246 programs that don't deserve federal funding. (Applause.) Some of them have noble titles, but none of them is indispensable. We can get rid of each and every one of them.

You know, it's time we rediscovered a home truth the American people have never forgotten: this government is too big and spends too much. (Applause.) And I call upon Congress to adopt a measure that will help put an end to the annual ritual of filling the budget with pork-barrel appropriations. Every year, the press has a field day making fun of outrageous examples – a Lawrence Welk museum, research grants for Belgian endive. We all know how these things get into the budget and maybe you need someone to help you say no. I know how to say it and I know what I need to make it stick. Give me the same thing 43 governors have, the line item veto, and let me help you control spending. (Applause.)

We must put an end to unfinanced federal government mandates. These are the requirements Congress puts on our cities, counties and states without supplying the money. If Congress passes a mandate, it should be forced to pay for it, and balance the cost with savings elsewhere. After all, a mandate just increases someone else's burden and that means higher taxes at the state and local level.

Step eight, Congress should enact the bold reform proposals that are still awaiting congressional action – bank reform, civil justice reform, tort reform, and my national energy strategy. (Applause.)

And finally, we must strengthen the family because it is the family that has the greatest bearing on our future. (Applause.) When Barbara holds an AIDS baby in her arms, and reads to children, she's saying to every person in this country, family matters.

And I am announcing tonight a new commission on America's Urban Families. I've asked Missouri's Governor John Ashcroft to be Chairman, former Dallas Mayor Ned Strauss to be Co-Chair. You know, I had mayors, the leading mayors from the League of Cities in the other day at the White House, and they told me something striking. They said that every one of them, Republican or Democrat, agreed on one thing: that the major cause of the problems of the cities is the dissolution of the family. They asked for this commission, and they were right to ask, because it's time to determine what we can do to keep families together, strong and sound. (Applause.)

There's one thing we can do right away, ease the burden of rearing a child. I ask you tonight to raise the personal exemption by $500 per child for every family. (Applause.) For a family with four kids, that's an increase of $2,000. This is a good start, in the right direction, and it's what we can afford.

It's time to allow families to deduct the interest they pay on student loans. (Applause.) I am asking you to do just that. And I'm asking you to allow people to use money from their IRAs to pay medical and education expenses – all without penalties. (Applause.)

And I'm asking for more. Ask American parents what they dislike about how things are going in our country, and chances are good that pretty soon they'll get to welfare. Americans are the most generous people on Earth. But we have to go back to the insight of Franklin Roosevelt who, when he spoke of what became the welfare program, warned that it must not become "a narcotic" and a "subtle destroyer" of the spirit.

Welfare was never meant to be a lifestyle; it was never meant to be a habit; it was never supposed to be passed from generation to generation like a legacy. It's time to replace the assumptions of the welfare state and help reform the welfare system. (Applause.)

States throughout the country are beginning to operate with new assumptions: that when able-bodied people receive government assistance, they have responsibilities to the taxpayer. A responsibility to seek work, education, or job training; a responsibility to get their lives in order; a responsibility to hold their families together and refrain from having children out of wedlock and a responsibility to obey the law.

We are going to help this movement. Often, state reform requires waiving certain federal regulations. I will act to make that process easier and quicker for every state that asks our help.

And I want to add, as we make these changes – we work together to improve this system – that our intention is not scapegoating or finger-pointing. If you read the papers or watch TV you know there's been a rise these days in a certain kind of ugliness, racist comments, anti-Semitism, an increased sense of division. Really, this is not us. This is not who we are. And this is not acceptable. (Applause.)

And so you have my plan for America. And I'm asking for big things, but I believe in my heart you will do what's right.

And you know, it's kind of an American tradition to show a certain skepticism toward our democratic institutions. I, myself, have sometimes thought the aging process could be delayed if it had to make its way through Congress. (Laughter and applause.) You will deliberate, and you will discuss, and that is fine. But, my friends, the people cannot wait. They need help now.

And there's a mood among us. People are worried. There's been talk of decline. Someone even said our workers are lazy and uninspired. And I thought, really? You go tell Neil Armstrong standing on the moon. Tell the men and women who put him there. Tell the American farmer who feeds his country and the world. Tell the men and women of Desert Storm. (Applause.)

Moods come and go, but greatness endures. Ours does. And maybe for a moment it's good to remember what, in the dailiness of our lives, we forget: We are still and ever the freest nation on Earth, the kindest nation on Earth, the strongest nation on Earth. And we have always risen to the occasion. (Applause.)

And we are going to lift this nation out of hard times inch by inch and day by day, and those who would stop us had better step aside. Because I look at hard times and I make this vow: This will not stand. (Applause.)

And so we move on together – a rising nation, the once and future miracle that is still, this night, the hope of the world.

Thank you. God bless you, and God bless our beloved country. Thank you very, very much. (Applause.)

This first trade edition of
"Read My Lips: No New Taxes"
is limited to 5,000 copies.

The paper is Wyoming Book
and the type is Garamond No. 3.

Edited by Dawn Hawkins,
Political Sciences Department,
Butte College.

First Trade Edition
produced under the direction of
Jack Bacon and Company,
Reno, Nevada.

Typography and design by
Jim Richards, Reno Typographers, Inc.

Printed by R. R. Donnelley & Sons
in the United States of America.